Lives Left Behind

10 Ukrainian Women in War and Peace

Ingrid Woodbridge

Lemberg Press
2019

To Jen and Mike,
awesome Emily's awesome
parents!

Merry Christmas
and Happy New Year.
Ingrid
Jan. 2021

Lemberg Press

L'viv, Ukraine

2019

Published in L'viv, Ukraine, by Lemberg Press.

Editors: Russell Woodbridge - Shawndee Edenfield - Karen Pearce

Page Designer: Ira-Rebeca @ Fiverr

ISBN ebook: 978-1-951730-01-7
ISBN paperback: 978-1-951730-00-0
ISBN audio book: 978-1-951730-02-4

http://ingridwoodbridge.com

Keywords: Ukraine - Women - War - Biography - Refugee - History

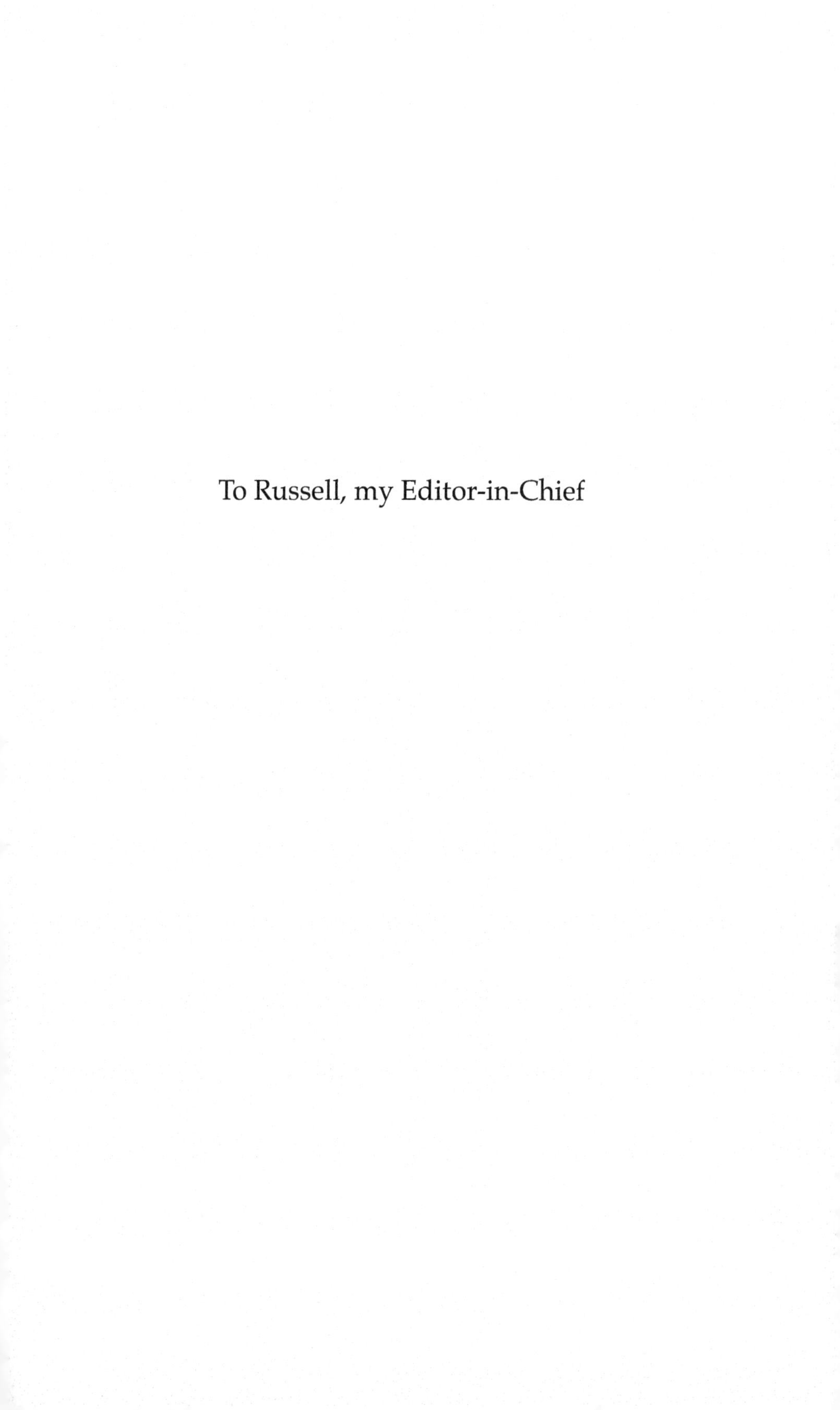

To Russell, my Editor-in-Chief

Lives Left Behind will cause you to experience the widest possible range of emotions. You will laugh and cry. You will feel despair but land in hope. And, you will see the mysterious, providential hand of God working behind the scenes for the good of His children. I am so grateful Ingrid Woodbridge has written this book. It needed to be written. I take great delight it commending it to you.

Dr. Daniel L. Akin, President, SEBTS

Why should you read *Lives Left Behind*? You need to know what God is doing around the world. From places you have heard about in world news, you will hear stories of grace that will move you to amazement and worship. In the lands formerly enclosed behind the iron curtain, a new day of God's grace has begun.

Dr. J.D. Greear, The Summit Church

Table of Contents

CHAPTER ONE

Introduction

In 2013, a revolution started in Kyiv, Ukraine, that impacted and forever changed the lives of the women in this story. In November 2013, the president of Ukraine pursued closer ties with Russia rather than signing the Ukraine-European Union Association Agreement. This sparked major demonstrations in the streets of Kyiv and led to the Maidan Revolution in 2014. Over 100 Ukrainians lost their lives in one day in Kyiv. Russia's annexation of Crimea happened in March 2014; severe unrest followed and the war in Eastern Ukraine started in late April 2014. The regions of Donbass and Lugansk, where these women are from, were taken over by the Russian-backed separatists.[1]

The separatists harassed and threatened Elisey Pronin, the senior pastor of the largest Baptist Church in the Lugansk region of Eastern Ukraine; the separatists burned down the Baptist church in August 2014. Elisey is now the pastor of the new *Disciples Church* in L'viv. His book, *Chronicles of Undeclared War*, describes the tragic events and how it affected his city, his congregation, and the individual church members.[2]

The women in *Lives Left Behind* are all connected. Most of them lived in the same city, Pervomaisk, in Eastern Ukraine and attended the Baptist church there. Interestingly, they all found their way to L'viv, Ukraine to start a new life and are now members at *Disciples Church,* a church plant started in 2016.

---

[1] To gain a better understanding of the events, I recommend the Netflix Documentation: Winter on Fire.

[2] Elisey Pronin, *Chronicles of Undeclared War* (Odessa, Ukraine: Takibook, 2017).

The women's lives are connected, even though their experiences are vastly different. Their stories are fascinating. Rita, Oksana, and Viola experienced their own dangers when the conflict started, but the bond between the grandmother, daughter, and granddaughter is stronger than ever. Sisters, Lena and Vika, were separated from their parents when the war started. Olya and her mother, Galina, never returned home from vacation. Ruslana helped Olya in Sunday School, and married Anton during the conflict while living in a camp for internally displaced peoples (IDP). Veronika sang in the church choir and saw the faithful example of her parents, Sergei and Valery, serving in the church. She ended up in L'viv via Poland on her escape from war-torn Eastern Ukraine. And Marina, from Crimea, left the area with her family just in time, finding her way to L'viv in amazing, yet often stressful ways. She shares the stories of her new friends at *Disciples Church* with a unique touch – fleeing from Russia with love.

Besides the city of L'viv and the church plant *Disciples Church*, one other connection is important to point out. All these women's lives are connected somehow to Ukrainian Baptist Theological Seminary (UBTS). Oksana's husband and Viola's dad, Elisey Pronin, graduated with his master degree from UBTS in partnership with Southeastern Baptist Theological Seminary in Wake Forest, NC, and works at UBTS as director of the church planting program. Rita is proud of her son-in-law. Olya is the administrative assistant to the Academic Dean. Ruslana is a graduate of UBTS, as is her husband Anton. Vika works in the finance office of the seminary, and Lena is a student in the international mission program. Veronika's husband Arthur was a student at UBTS, and Marina's husband Dima gives music lessons in the music department. The seminary has helped many of these families resettle.

Why did I write this book? And why should you read it? These are really good questions. I live in L'viv, Ukraine. My husband, Russell, and I are part of *Disciples Church*, and Elisey Pronin is our pastor. The women you are going to read about are all at our church plant, so I know them personally, and have listened to their amazing stories in awe and wonder. I had a strong sense that their stories should be told. The war in Eastern Ukraine is still going on. The events described in this book are very much near and present experiences, not something from a distant past.

By God's grace, I enjoy writing and researching. Praying about the title, the idea of *Lives Left Behind* came to my mind, and so the writing journey began. I prepared the questions for the interviews and chose the women. Then I conducted the interviews in Russian, and translated and transcribed their testimonies into English. These are their stories told by themselves.

Why should you read this book? You need to know what is going on in the world, even if it is far away from your place of living. Your knowledge of true events will hopefully move you to actions in some way. Praying for the region and the conflict, creating awareness in your circle of influence, and helping in some practical ways would all be great action steps for you to take after reading this book.[3]

Enjoy reading *Lives Left Behind*.

Ingrid Woodbridge

November 2019

L'viv, Ukraine

---

[3] Other resources I recommend for further reading are: www.kyivpost.com and www.baptyst.com/ukrainian-postman.

The city of Pervomaisk is located 50 km south of Severodonetsk.

CHAPTER TWO

Oksana

Oksana was born in Pervomaisk, in the Lugansk Region of Eastern Ukraine on December 12, 1977. She grew up in an apartment in the center of town. Her home was near the elementary school; the kindergarten and some stores were within walking distance of her house. It was very comfortable to live there, she recalls. Her parents had also grown up in this city. Her father, Alexey, was born in 1950, and her mom, Rita, in 1958. Oksana has a sister, Jana, who is three-and-a-half years older. Oksana described her childhood as very idyllic. "We had a great family, we lived close to each other – even two grandmothers lived nearby, and our home town was pretty and peaceful and quiet."

Oksana had many friends in town. She spent the summer holidays mostly with her grandmother Rita, who had a small home and a big yard. The kids played often in the quiet streets of the town, used their bicycles to get around, and worked in the family's potato fields. Oksana's family would also take a vacation every year and travel to the sea. These trips would be either to the Azov Sea or the Black Sea around Crimea. One time the family even traveled to Sochi in Russia.

Oksana remembers some major world events happening during her childhood. First was Chernobyl, the nuclear disaster in 1986. She remembers the news and headlines. Everyone was talking about the nuclear meltdown, but she did not understand all the details or the impact on the country. She was nine years old when it happened. She also remembers the sequence of events that led to the break-up of the Soviet Union and how Ukraine became an independent country in Eastern Europe in 1991.

After finishing high school, Oksana studied for two years at the medical college, from 1996-1998, and became a nurse. Holidays were celebrated in typical Ukrainian family tradition. The whole clan would get together, there would be a lot of food spread out on the tables, and they would celebrate. Religious holidays were not observed at all in the Kiyan home. At this time, Oksana's father was the only one going to the local Baptist church, which was considered by many to be a cult or sect. Rita, Oksana's mother, was an Orthodox believer, but she and her daughters stayed home on Sundays. Only on the really big Christian holidays, like Easter and Christmas, would the whole family go with Oksana's father to his Baptist church.

Oksana's faith testimony begins with her reflection of her dad attending the local Baptist church regularly. He was a deacon there, but her mom went very rarely to church. Oksana and her sister occasionally went to Sunday School with her dad. But as a teenager, Oksana considered church boring and stayed away. She did not really understand what church was all about. The impressions she had about church were that the church was small, the preachers were old, there was nothing appealing to a teenager, the sermons were long, and the messages were not understandable. Oksana did not know who God was. Initially, she thought that maybe the speaker in the pulpit was God! Her life revolved around going to discos for dancing, enjoying close girlfriends, and living a free life. Still, on holidays, she would try to go with her father to church, just to please him.

When she was eighteen years old and had just finished high school, the Baptist church in Pervomaisk started building a new auditorium for the congregation. The location of the new building was in the center of town, close to Oksana's home. Her father, by this time already in retirement, built the church structure with his own hands, stone by stone. As the church moved into her neighborhood, Oksana went more often to church events. She listened more to the Word of God being shared at church, and slowly the Word of God convicted her. She began to understand what the church was all about, who God was, and who she was in relation to Him.

There was one sermon that really touched her heart. The preacher made the point that if there is a heaven, then there is also a hell. The preacher stated that God requires a decision for or against Him by every individual. Despite the fact that most people try to stay neutral or noncommittal, this is not an option with God. Oksana knew that she was trying to live in that neutral place, believing in God, but not having made a commitment to Him. This sermon was the turning point for her.

She repented and invited God to be her Lord and Savior. She was nineteen years old when she became a follower of Jesus in February 1997. To affirm her decision publicly, Oksana went forward at the end of the service and prayed with the pastor. After the service, her father greeted her, saying, "Welcome to the family of God!" Her dad was happy about Oksana's decision, having prayed for her for a long time. Oksana followed her public faith declaration with believer's baptism in July 1997. The happy continuation of this testimony is that Rita, her mom, accepted Christ six months later.

After her salvation, Oksana began to fellowship more intentionally with the youth group at church. [Youth Group in Ukraine is fifteen to thirty years old.] They sang and made music, had good fellowship, and got to know each other deeply. Oksana was initially just a consistent participant, but after several months, the pastor came to her and asked her to work in the church's Sunday School program. Oksana thought she was not ready or prepared for such a task, but the pastor's words were very affirming. He told her boldly, "You are ready to serve." So, Oksana began to lead a Sunday School group, and these young children became like her own kids. Olya Kiyan, whose story is in chapter four, was one member of this Sunday School class.

Oksana, having finished medical college, worked as a nurse full time by 1998, but every moment of free time she spent preparing for the Sunday School lessons at church. She also started singing in the choir of the Baptist church, as she really enjoyed music. So, her life was filled and fulfilled with work and voluntary ministry opportunities.

Oksana sees the hand of God in this season of her life, because earlier she had wanted to live for herself and do only what she wanted to do. But from the time of her salvation, her desires changed and she wanted to serve God with all her heart. "God did a mighty work in my heart and mind, changing my desires, giving me strength and wisdom to do ministry and joy in serving others." Oksana said that she learned then to trust God completely for her life, no matter what was coming. And what was coming was her future husband, Elisey Pronin.

Elisey arrived at the church about two months after Oksana started to attend regularly. Elisey had become a believer at the age of eighteen, and God had completely captured his heart. He was looking for a place to serve and minister. Oksana and Elisey met frequently and got acquainted at church events.

Oksana liked a lot of things about Elisey: he had strong leadership skills, he was very personable and friendly, he had musical skills, and back then he even had hair! "Elisey is bald and handsome now!" she said. Elisey organized children's and youth outings to the lake, to the sea, and to the forest. Together they served in the youth group and had many opportunities to get to know each other better and observe one another in ministry. During the hot months of 1998, Oksana and Elisey led summer camps together for all ages.

In December of 1998, Elisey proposed to Oksana. Interestingly enough, Oksana took two days to give Elisey her answer. Elisey told her if she said no, he would move to Irpin, near Kyiv, for some ministry position. But Oksana gave a joyful yes to Elisey's proposal and they became engaged. They immediately planned the wedding for the following spring. But, as they did not really want to wait, they had the wedding just two months later, in January of 1999. The wedding festivities took place at the Baptist church in Pervomaisk. Life for believers in small towns like Pervomaisk centered around the local Baptist church.

Oksana jokes about her relationship to Elisey, saying that they did not have a long, romantic dating relationship; they just got married, and it has been romantic since then. Oksana and Elisey have been married now for over twenty years. The couple has two children. Their daughter Viola was born in 2000 (her story is in chapter three in *Lives Left Behind*). Oksana explained that they chose the name Viola because they really liked it and it was an unusual name in Ukraine. With their son, David, they chose a biblical name because they liked the character of David in the Scripture. Raising the children, working, and doing ministry was the normal rhythm of their lives.

Oksana reflected back over a regular week back in Pervomaisk, when all was still calm and peaceful. She was busy with two little children. Viola was a young school girl when baby David joined the family, and, Oksana remembered with a smile, David needed a lot of attention. Part of their day was spent at the local Baptist church where Elisey had become pastor in 2007. There was always some ministry going on.

One interesting ministry Oksana took part in was inviting young mothers to church with their children. The church had a big back yard where the children could play and the moms could fellowship over tea and cookies. Oksana was also involved in the youth ministry, she hosted a home group, and sang in the choir. Since Elisey was the senior pastor, a lot was expected from Oksana as the pastor's wife. Elisey would often invite people to their home, and Oksana would serve refreshments or meals for the guests. Life was enjoyable, comfortable and peaceful, but changes were coming.

The conflict in the East started with protests in Kyiv, the capital of Ukraine, in November 2013. The Ukrainian president, Yanukovych, had halted EU association agreement negotiations under political pressure from Russia. In response, the Ukrainian people peacefully demonstrated in the streets of Kyiv. On November 30, 2013, the general prosecutor ordered the police to clear Maidan Nesalezhnosti [Independence Square] in Kyiv, where thousands of protesters had assembled. The government's aggressive violence against their own people was shocking and captured on video for all to see.

The protesters endured months of clashes with the police, standing in rain and snow against a corrupt system. They endured until February 2014. Then snipers, trained security forces of the government, were stationed on key buildings around Independence Square and fired into the crowd of protesters, killing and wounding hundreds of defenseless victims. The voice of the people rose in response to these atrocities. A full revolution was now underway in Ukraine, and the world was watching. The consequential unfolding events would directly and dramatically affect Oksana and Elisey Pronin in Pervomaisk, far in the east of Ukraine.

The ousted president of Ukraine fled to Russia. By March 2014 Russian forces annexed Crimea. By April 2014 pro-Russian armed groups seized parts of the Donetsk and Lugansk regions. The war had come to the Pronin's doorstep.

Normally, the large and active Baptist church served the community with many ministries. Staff and volunteers at the rehabilitation center helped addicts break free from alcohol and narcotics. Small groups met for Bible study and prayer, and many people were involved in serving the city and the church family. All was going well, and life was wonderful in small town Ukraine. Every day, life centered around activities of the church. Oksana remembered that they had planned a children's camp for the summer of 2014.

Suddenly, war started in the neighboring town. They heard the sounds of artillery, and their windows vibrated from the impact of bombs. They fled into the basement of the house for safety and protection, not knowing how close the bombing would come to their town. Soldiers and police appeared in town suddenly, questioning people and examining their documents. Ukrainian mercenaries formed bands to seize control of the streets. These were criminals who formed a kind of mafia, with self-imposed power and rule. Oksana felt a lot of fear and anxiety about what was going on. Elisey's account of the events and emotions during this traumatic time are recorded in his book *Chronicles of Undeclared War*.[4]

The youth group from church, around twenty teens, had already left for a camp in Kyiv called 'Word of Life'. Oksana's daughter Viola was part of that group. Many people expected the unrest to be over in about a week, but intense fighting continued. Elisey and Oksana called the youth group and informed their leaders that the situation was too unstable to return. The group needed to stay at Word of Life camp. This one-extra-week-stay turned into several months for the youth group.

At the church in Pervomaisk, Elisey made many phone calls to churches outside the war zone, asking who could receive church members if they wanted to leave Pervomaisk. At this point in the conflict, not many people wanted to leave their home area, because they did not understand how serious or how long-lasting this conflict would be. Everybody expected the fighting to last a few weeks at best, Oksana said. Everyone still hoped to return to some form of normalcy. No one understood the real danger. On the radio, citizens were told that the conflict and the fighting would not come to their city, that everything was under control, and therefore, there was no need to leave the city. They were told not to fear and not to make plans for an evacuation.

But Elisey saw things differently. He encouraged families, and especially moms with children, to find ways and opportunities to leave the city and go somewhere safe, even if it was just temporary. The Baptist church in Vinnytsia invited thirty adults plus their children to come and be temporary guests of the church at the small church-owned camp site. Normally, summer camps were held in this wooded area. Now it became one of the first refugee camps. [Technically, war-affected Ukrainians who remained in country are called internally displaced persons (IDP's), but for simplicity, I will call them refugees.] Elisey bought the train tickets on the internet. The following day, this large group left Pervomaisk. It was a hot July day in 2014. Many of

---

[4] Elisey Pronin, *Chronicles of Undeclared War* (Odessa, Ukraine: Takibook, 2017).

these people would never return to their home town. Oksana and her son David were part of this exodus. Elisey stayed behind, helping other members of the church to leave town. He also provided local assistance to people who wanted to stay and wait it out.

The travelers only got as far as Kyiv when news reached them that Pervomaisk was now also in the war zone. The battle scenario and the conflict had reached their beloved small town, after all. At this point, no one else was able or allowed to leave the city of Pervomaisk. This first group had escaped, but what uncertain future did their loved ones left behind now face?

Once the women and children arrived in Kyiv, they were able to call their husbands. They found out that war was happening on their streets, the sound of bombing was a reality in their city, people were in lockdown, and their husbands were pinned down in a city in turmoil. It was horrible news for the travelers. The refugees traveled onward and soon arrived and settled into the camp in Vinnytsia as well as they could. Their thoughts were constantly on those left behind in Pervomaisk.

To manage the situation in Pervomaisk, Christian brothers would move together into several homes to stick together through this crisis. In Oksana's home, four men lived with Pastor Elisey. Their house had a large, solid basement, where Elisey hosted up to thirty people during the bomb raids, many of them neighbors of the Pronin family. They would read the Bible together, pray, and sing praise songs, focusing on God, not the gruesome war reality outside. It was an amazing opportunity for evangelism, Oksana stated, because people were afraid for their lives and sought answers to serious life questions.

Things did not get better; they actually got worse. Periodic short cease-fires would enable people to evacuate the war zone. Since the city did not provide any buses or transports for their citizens, it was only through the common effort of the believers that people were able to leave when the cease-fire was announced. It was difficult for the men in the church to find out when the evacuation windows would open up. For three months, Elisey organized convoys of cars for those church members who wanted to leave Pervomaisk.

Many people, at this point, wanted to leave, but they could not bring any of their belongings – not even beloved pets – on the westward journey. Every seat in every car was needed for people to sit, to squeeze together to get out of the war zone. Even though people came to the meeting point with suitcases, all of these had to be left behind in order to fit as many people in each car as possible. When the cease fire became effective, people were allowed to drive out in these convoys.

Additionally, people were encouraged to just walk out of town in a group of pedestrians, using the opportunity to leave the city any way they could. Some people in the broader area of Pervomaisk did not leave, some due to health problems, some due to a false hope of a short conflict. Many were simply too afraid to start a new life in another part of Ukraine. As much as was possible, the Pronin family and their church helped elderly and disabled people leave the war zone. But many of them wanted to stay, hoping for their old normal lives to return.

The people who left Pervomaisk in these convoys gathered in a nearby town called Severodonetsk at a very old church. The refugees began to group together to try to establish some order and structure to their temporary living situation since they were now refugees in their own country. All kinds of people mingled together in this camp, believers and unbelievers, men, women, and children. Anyone who wanted to leave the war zone and could, did at this point, leaving behind their lives in Pervomaisk.

Ultimately, Elisey and his Baptist men organized three refugee camps and provided for the humanitarian needs of the temporary citizens. The pastor and his men travelled back and forth to and from Pervomaisk whenever a cease fire would allow them access. Oksana lived during this initial time with her son David in the Vinnytsia refugee camp. Viola was still with the youth group at Word of Life camp outside of Kyiv. For five weeks, the Vinnytsia camp was home, shelter, communication center, and hope to Oksana.

Then Elisey moved his family to Severodonetsk. This city was in the Ukrainian territory of the war zone. Elisey felt it was important for the family to be together again, even though it meant being closer to the danger. Oksana did not agree with this move. She cried a lot and became hysterical at times, remembering that during this time she was very scared and anxious. They lived so close to the conflict zone, they could hear the artillery, feel the bombs falling, and observe the raids by airplanes. They lived in dread and heard the rumble of tanks on the streets.

Oksana recalled that they lived temporarily on the seventh floor of a building. As she was looking outside, she could see tanks and war vehicles amass. These were Ukrainian military convoys heading to the war zone. She understood that these convoys were heading to her city where people she knew in her town would suffer and die. War had come to their hometown. Oksana also feared that the war would creep ever closer, and what this evening at bedtime was Ukraine, might be Russia in the morning when she woke up.

But their move to Severodonetsk meant that they could minister to people in greater need than they. From Severodonetsk the family provided logistical help and support to other refugees. They would travel back and forth to the camps, which the Pervomaisk Baptist church had started.

The situation in the villages was worsening. In the first few months of the conflict, it was still possible to bring fresh produce into the war zone from neighboring towns. It was like the Berlin Air Bridge during the Cold War, but this humanitarian aid lift was happening between towns in Eastern Ukraine. Now the people often had no food, no fresh water, no clothes, and none of the stores were open anymore for business.

This lack of clothes also affected Oksana and her family. They left Pervomaisk in July of 2014 with summer clothes for a week, anticipating and hoping to return to their homes soon. Now they had been on the road and living in temporary shelters and camps for more than four months already. Oksana had one suitcase for all of the family's belongings. It was a really stressful and challenging time. But she joked, saying, "At least we could grab this one suitcase quickly and leave if we had to escape again."

Living like this for months on end was a really difficult time in Oksana's life. The practical aspects of residing in a refugee camp and, afterwards, moving into temporary housing close to the war zone, can only be imagined. The memories were hard for Oksana to share.

Viola, Oksana's daughter, had by now returned from Kyiv to join the family again. They lived then in Severodonetsk and Viola was enrolled in school for the fall of 2014. The war had begun in the summer of 2014, but by fall all the children had to go to school somewhere. Viola did not like school in this city; it was a huge stressor for her. Viola simply could not get used to the new situation. She was fifteen years old and was experiencing war and all its horrors in her most formative years. The family lived through this season of life with stress, anxiety, and fear. Each day was clouded with a sense of disbelief about the actual events, which were affecting their lives so dramatically.

Before the conflict, the Baptist church in Pervomaisk had often hosted American teams for summer camps. Because of this, Elisey was considered an American spy by the occupiers of the town! Elisey had good relationships with the US churches sending these teams. Two frequent team members, Dan and Susan, had invited the Pronin family to visit them in the States even prior to the breakout of war, but Elisey had always said that he could not leave the local church. Now Dan and Susan urged the family to come to the US to rest and be refreshed after their stressful war experiences. At first, Elisey insisted he could not ignore the needs of his people in such a crisis, so the Pronins had stayed nearby when war broke out. Elsey did everything in his power to help local believers and be a testimony to those who had no understanding of a Christian perspective on life.

Now the needs of his own family became apparent to Elisey, as stress had taken a major toll on all of them. The Pronins applied for visas and received them from the US embassy. They understood this as a sign from God that they were all, including Elisey, to go to the US for a while together. At this point, Elisey and Oksana reasoned, life in the refugee camps was firmly established and functioning as well as could be expected given the circumstances. People had their own space (huts on the premises of the camp) and there was a church team in place, responsible for helping and providing for these three camps. Financial aid was also coming in regularly to help the people in the camps. Elisey believed he could step away from these camp responsibilities, and so the family decided to leave for the US in November 2014.

Oksana recalled that when they got to America, they kissed the ground, they were so happy and relieved to be in safety. After having experienced war for so many months, it was a new freedom and lightness they suddenly felt. The danger was gone, the fear fell off like a coat, they could breathe easy and hope again. She said with their arrival in the US, their rehabilitation began. They lived in Louisburg, Kansas, for nine months. Pastor Dan and his wife Susan wanted to do anything and everything for them to help them in their recuperation. They rented an apartment for them, bought them things for living, brought fruits and other groceries. They often ate together, talked, and relaxed. It was truly rehabilitating. "We were getting better and healthier," Oksana recalled.

Elisey had many opportunities to speak at churches, schools, colleges, and social clubs like Rotary, sharing with people about the war in Eastern Ukraine. The family met many new friends, people who showed genuine interest in the events around the Donbass region. But Oksana cautioned by saying, "Even though this interest was great, it was also difficult to accommodate, because in the retelling of the events you relive everything that has happened, and so, the trauma continues."

Oksana and Elisey were able to Skype with friends and family members in Eastern Ukraine occasionally, given the difficult situation and the technological challenges. They regularly received updates on what was going on and what needed to get done. They were able to raise support for the people in the war zone.

While staying in contact with the people of the East, it became apparent to Elisey that more needed to be done for them. He constantly thought about ideas to help the residents of the war zone who were caught in a very hard place. American churches could do more to help these suffering Ukrainians. The Pronins were invited to stay long term in the US. Oksana really wanted to continue living in America. It was a place of safety and security. The church in Kansas had helped them so much to establish a new life. The children, David and Viola, had attended local schools, learning English; they were adjusting to the American way of life. Elisey had begun serving in a local church as assistant pastor. But it had never been the family's plan to stay in the US; they had always just considered this time an opportunity to be refreshed and revived after their traumatic experiences of war.

Elisey did listen to God's voice. And although they could have stayed in the US and lived their new, comfortable, safe life, they returned to Ukraine, their home country, in the summer of 2015. It was a huge decision, bathed in prayer, joy, and sadness.

For their daughter Viola, the return to Ukraine was especially difficult. Oksana reflected on the decision to come back to Ukraine. Returning to Pervomaisk was obviously not an option. But Elisey had received an invitation to work at the seminary in L'viv, Ukrainian Baptist Theological Seminary (UBTS). God had put a divine time line in place to move the Pronin family to L'viv. Slavik Pyzh, president of UBTS since 2014, and Elisey knew each other already. Slavik had heard about the many ministries Elisey and his church were doing in Crimea and in the Donbass region. Even before the family left for their sabbatical time in the US, Slavik extended an invitation to Elisey to work at UBTS.

Another influencing factor in considering L'viv for work and life was a conversation the Pronins had with Sasha Savich, pastor of a Baptist church in Lutsk at that time. Sasha translated at a family conference in Kyiv, interpreting for the American speakers. The Pronin family attended this conference in September 2014. Sasha took time to ask Elisey and Oksana some very important questions: What are you going to do? Where will you serve? Where will you live? Sasha knew that Slavik was looking for help at the Baptist seminary in L'viv. They should consider it as a possibility. Then, several months later while the family was living in Kansas, came the renewed invitation from Slavik to Elisey to work at UBTS. But Slavik made it clear, that Elisey was free to choose.

Oksana remembered how the children felt about leaving America and returning to Ukraine. She said with a laugh that Viola and David definitely did not want to leave Kansas. Viola cried and cried and even beseeched Pastor Dan to keep her in the US and to talk to her father about staying. At this point, Viola really liked her school, she had settled in well with new friends, and she liked everything American. David was very little when the family left Ukraine, and all he said from his limited memory was, "Everything in America is better." Even though David was young, he picked up on the differences between the two countries, telling his mom that in America everything was cleaner, easier, and more comfortable than back home.

Reflecting back on the situation in the East, Oksana said that by this time they had no family or relatives remaining in the occupied zone. Initially, her parents had stayed in Pervomaisk with Elisey when the war broke out, but they left in due time. Elisey's mom had evacuated with Oksana in July 2014, to escape the unrest and live at the refugee camp in Vinnytsia. Elisey's father had stayed a little bit longer, but ultimately, he, too, had left for safety and freedom in non-occupied regions of Ukraine. The rest of their relatives had exited when Elisey organized the car convoys during the cease fire. So, no one stayed behind, but their lives were left behind forever.

Oksana explained her emotional processing, her feelings and thoughts about the whole situation at the end of the interview. She said that at the beginning of all the troubles, it was a time of great sadness and difficulty. It was physically, mentally, and emotionally exhausting. It was truly traumatic, the hardest experience of her life. Eventually, through the weeks and months of the ever-increasing conflict, Oksana understood that she needed to embrace and use the new situation and make the best out of it. She had to say final and hard goodbyes – to her home and to her town, to everything that was familiar and known. She had to accept that her old life was to be left behind.

Prayerfully they made the decision to move back to Ukraine. Oksana said that when they arrived in L'viv in 2015, it was difficult for her at the beginning. Elisey began right away his work at UBTS, so he was gone the whole day. Oksana stayed at home with the children in a new, unfamiliar city. David and Viola should be going to school, but it was difficult to figure out when and where school would happen. She did not know where stores were in her new neighborhood, where to buy fresh produce, and how to do life in L'viv. She admitted to crying a lot and falling into a deep depression about her new life.

The Pronins also did not have many family members or friends around them at this point, as they were one of the first families to relocate to L'viv. Eventually, Anton and Ruslana, together with Olya Kiyan, arrived in L'viv, following the invitation of the Pronin family for a new life in Western Ukraine. (Olya's and Ruslana's stories follow in chapters four and five of *Lives Left Behind.*) After a while, other friends, Sergey and his wife Valery, arrived with their family. Elisey advocated for many of these folks with Slavik at the seminary, to give them work, so that they all could start a new life and support themselves.

Elisey and Oksana began hosting a small group for Bible study and prayer in their home in the fall of 2015. The participants were all refugees from Pervomaisk. The group was very small, but the bond of shared experiences that tied them together was strong. Everybody was in the same situation, trying to build a new life in L'viv after having lost everything in the East. It took close to a year to adapt to this new city, this new life, this new situation. The idea was eventually born to start a new church here in L'viv; this would be a second wing of ministry for Elisey, in addition to his seminary work. A key factor for the church plant would be to provide humanitarian aid to the many refugees arriving in L'viv. The strategy was to provide substantial humanitarian packages to these people and build relationships, inviting them to the small group, with the idea that the small group would eventually become a church.

The plan worked. Many people thankfully accepted the humanitarian goods provided by the ministry of Elisey's small group. Attendance at the Bible study rose to such a level that a meeting room had to be found to host the gathering. Elisey approached Slavik and "rented" the UBTS library for Sunday afternoon church services.

Initially the meeting was still structured like a small group setting, sitting around a table, drinking tea, sharing life, studying the Bible, Elisey giving a short sermon, everyone then sharing prayer requests.

But as the group grew, Elisey organized the assembly into a more formal congregation, having a praise and worship band leading through the service, technology supporting the music and the life of the church through announcements and videos, and guest speakers becoming part of the preaching rotation. Oksana said that this formation of what is now called *Disciples Church* is one of the greatest blessings of the entire experience.

Back in Pervomaisk, she reflected, there were about 300 people at the church. When Elisey joined the pastoral staff, ministries and working teams were already in place, many people came regularly, the church functioned well, and was known in the community. But to start something new, a new church plant, was an opportunity to see God at work in new ways, Oksana said.

In this new endeavor, a financial budget had to be drawn up, leaders had to be trained, the course for church membership had to be developed, teams for different aspects of ministry had to be formed. Even though Oksana could not quite envision this small group becoming a church, God had big, amazing plans. God was doing something far beyond anything they could have imagined (Ephesians 3:20). And now there is a new church in L'viv, called *Disciples Church*. About eighty people currently attend on any Sunday and Elisey has a team of pastors and deacons serving with him. Oksana is a wonderful, godly woman. She manages her home and household well, and is helping her husband, ministering together at *Disciples Church*.

A final blessing that Oksana mentioned was their new apartment. To avoid paying rent for the next years, they were able to borrow money and they bought a small, two-room place in a new neighborhood of L'viv. They now pay back installments like rent, but with the result of having their own place in the city center.

Viola and David share one room, Oksana hosts the ladies Bible study group on Wednesdays in her kitchen, and they meet many of their neighbors on the playground and the adjoining soccer field in an effort to get to know the lost around them. Oksana said, yes, it is a very small apartment for the four of them, plus a bunny and a cat (and occasionally kittens!), but it is their own place; that makes it special.

After having lost everything due to the war, to now own a place in L'viv feels like a miracle. "I saw God blessing us and meeting our needs in amazing ways," Oksana said. Viola is now attending college in L'viv and David is attending the local elementary school. "I cannot imagine how God would have worked in our lives had we stayed in America, but I see His blessings on our life here and now - and I am thankful. God loves us and He blesses obedience. Of that I am sure," she added. She said that she feels calm and peaceful now, her heart is at rest, she is not depressed or worried or anxious anymore. She feels well, she said, because God gave her calmness and inner peace.

But not all is well in her world, because there is still a war going on in Ukraine, the country is in conflict, there are occupied territories, and people still suffer. Her final comment in the interview was, "We need to pray for Ukraine."

CHAPTER THREE

Rita

Rita Kiyan is Oksana's mother. She was born in 1958 in Pervomaisk and grew up in the Lugansk region. Her Ukrainian mother came from Cherkasy; her Russian father grew up in Volgograd. Rita finished school in Pervomaisk. She said she experienced a happy and carefree childhood in a small Ukrainian village.

She married very young. Rita met her future husband, Alexey, in a taxi. Though they lived near each other, they had never met, until they flagged down the same taxi. He was several years older than Rita. They dated for a little while, then decided to get married. She was fifteen years old when she married Alexey in 1974.

By the time Rita was sixteen, she had her first daughter Jana, and three and a half years later, her daughter Oksana was born. Rita was nineteen years young and had two children. Her little girls kept this young mom busy. Rita's husband worked in the coal mines of the Lugansk region. He was on a technical team for the mine and managed his own schedule, as well as supervising workers under him.

Rita recalled a moving story connected to the mine. One weekend in 1977, Alexey was off from work. Rita's mom, living in Cherkasy, sent a telegram informing them that she was feeling unwell and asking them to come. Rita and Alexey left rather quickly and drove to Cherkasy. The road trip took about seven hours. That weekend, a terrible accident happened at the mine. The lift crashed into the mine, and sixty people perished. Most of Alexey's group of workers died in that accident. If Alexey had been there, Rita believes, he would have been killed for sure. Rita's mom's health quickly improved and she was on the road to recovery. Looking back now at this scenario, Rita considers this to be the first time the hand of God protected their lives.

During this time, neither Rita nor Alexey were believers. Rita explained that they were agnostics, because they would have said, "Yes, there is a God." They never had doubts about God's existence. But they were not Christians even though Alexey actually grew up in Christian family.

Her children, Jana and Oksana, grew up during the 1980s and 1990s in Pervomaisk. Alexey worked in the mine and Rita also worked for a time in the mining company, but her job was in the office, not in the dangerous shafts. In the 1990s, which were difficult years for the Ukrainian economy, Rita worked in a grocery store temporarily, supplementing their family income. She had also trained with a good hair dresser to become a professional friseur. She finished special courses in hair coloring and received a diploma.

Soon afterwards, her neighbor in Pervomaisk opened up a beauty salon and invited Rita to join her as hair dresser and coloring expert. Rita really liked this salon and was a skilled hair dresser. She worked there for many years and it was a wonderful time, reflected Rita. The salon became the best and most prestigious beauty salon in Pervomaisk. The clients were nice, educated, and cultured, and they appreciated the decent prices at the professional salon. The city was small, and no one made a lot of money. At this time, about 40,000 people lived in Pervomaisk.

Oksana and Jana played a lot on the streets of Pervomaisk with other kids. They went to kindergarten, elementary school, and secondary school. In their free time, they played in the woods. The girls even joined the children's play group at a church. Rita would always try to be home when her daughters came home from school. She managed all the housework, the cooking and the cleaning, and supervised her daughters' homework. Her work at the beauty salon was always part-time, Rita mentioned, so she could be there for her children.

After the traumatic event at the mine in 1977 Alexey repented of his sin against God, and became a Christian. So many of his friends and colleagues had died. Only a relationship with Jesus gave hope and perspective at such a time as this, he thought. But Rita would not follow his decision to become a Christian. She waited.

Alexey started attending church regularly, not just on Sundays, but during the week, too. He often invited his wife and his daughters to go with him. But they would always decline. They wanted to stay home and relax. They were a fairly typical family. Rita thought that it was good enough to believe in God in general terms. She was busy with the children and with her work at the salon. She watched her husband go to church three times a week.

Alexey became really involved in the ministry of the Baptist church to the point where he practically worked at the church full-time, in addition to his full-time job at the mine. Rita thought, "I don't need that; I believe in God. I am good. I am busy."

At home, there were not too many conflicts, Rita said, even though she was not a believer and Alexey was. Rita watched the new life her husband lived. Rita knew for herself, that she always believed in God. But she considered it unnecessary to go to church. Her thought was that "everyone can make up his own mind about what to believe and what to do about his beliefs." The local church was very conservative in Rita's view. She watched it and decided she did not like it. But God kept working in her life.

Rita's mom eventually died, prompting a thinking process in Rita's mind about grief, loss and eternal life. Her daughter Oksana had recently become a believer whose life was clearly changing from selfishness to acts of service. Rita, still skeptical, began to go to church, and she listened and kept listening to the word of God. She heard in the messages that a person cannot keep the Law, that repentance and confession brought new life, and that believer's baptism was the public step to then become a member of the church. She did not want to take the first step, but eventually she repented - at the age of thirty-nine. The year was 1997, and Rita had waited twenty years to make the same decision Alexey had made, professing her personal faith in Jesus Christ.

But God had even greater plans in mind for Rita. Alexey, her husband, became the pastor of the Baptist church in Pervomaisk in 2001, when the current pastor of the Baptist church suddenly decided to move to Kyiv to start a new ministry. For nine years, Alexey had served as a deacon in the church. He built the church building literally stone by stone. He was involved from the first stone to the last brick, and rejoiced when the dome was put into place. During his time as a deacon, Alexey would work in the mine at night; during the day he would work at the church; and in-between, he would study theology. Alexey finished pastoral studies at an institute, and the church called him to be the new pastor. Alexey served for six years as senior pastor and Rita became a pastor's wife. Surprise! "God's ways are indeed mysterious!" she laughed.

Rita's ministry focused on hospitality, organizing luncheons during the building phase of the church for all the workers, and hosting groups in her home for Bible study. During this time, Elisey Pronin was already a member of the church. The Baptist church, consisting of about 400 members, organized teams and groups working for the good of the community. Evangelism was a vital part of the church's ministry. The church also established a rehabilitation ministry and provided humanitarian aid to those in need. They even started a home for orphans.

Rita's daughter Jana married and had a baby, but continued to attend the medical college. Oksana was still in eleventh grade. Rita recounted that everyone helped to take care of baby Christina – there was a line-up of helpers. Oksana married Elisey in 1999 when she was twenty years old. Elisey was still a student and Oksana worked as a nurse in the local clinic. Everyone had moved to their own apartments, but they all stayed in the same town. Pervomaisk was home, after all. They enjoyed close relationships and stayed in close contact with each another. Rita now has four grandchildren. Jana's daughters are Christina (born 1992) and Eva (born 2000). Oksana and Elisey have Viola (born 2000) and David (born 2009). When Viola was born, Rita would help every day with the baby. She would walk her granddaughter in the stroller, and Viola would nap at her grandma's home. Over time, a close relationship developed. Rita and Viola are very close to this day.

At Alexey's retirement from the church in 2007, their son-in-law, Elisey Pronin, became the senior pastor. The ministry expanded over the next years and the church grew. Rita's husband stayed on at the church as an elder. Then the war started. There had been political demonstrations in Kyiv for months, since November 2013, but the capital was far away from homey Pervomaisk. Now, however, the conflict had spread to the Eastern regions of Ukraine.

Initially, the war began in the spring of 2014 in Slovyansk, a town far away from Pervomaisk. Everyone in town believed that the war would not come to Pervomaisk, Rita said, because the fighting was really far away, and the conflict would probably soon be over. They told each other not to be afraid; this was just a little uprising, and it would end shortly. No one was ready for what was to happen.

The front came ever closer to Pervomaisk. Soldiers and police appeared overnight, checking documents, questioning pedestrians, stopping vehicles. Elisey decided that his family needed to leave town, so they prepared to evacuate in July 2014. Elisey helped Oksana, Jana, and the younger children to leave town on the train, while the separatists and occupiers arrived with tanks and military equipment.

Rita and Alexey stayed in Pervomaisk, unwilling to leave at this point. Elisey also stayed in his apartment after the successful evacuation of his own family. Rita received a message from the manager at the beauty salon, stating that the salon would open that July day despite the apparent unrest. She called all her customers, explained to them what was happening, but indicated that they still would service the scheduled appointments. Only Rita and one other lady who did manicures arrived for work that day. Rita managed to provide some haircuts and color, but it became increasingly dangerous in town. A nearby explosion shook the floor of the salon as the glass windows vibrated. They quickly closed the salon.

Rita wanted to get home to Alexey. As she was taking a shortcut through the park toward her apartment, she saw airplanes flying across the area and she heard anti-aircraft guns firing. She made it home, frightened, anxious, and disturbed. The next eight days were spent inside, in lockdown. Their building had no basement, so they lay on the floor in the corridor, which had no windows, and endured one air raid after another.

The internet was still working for a few days, so Rita and Alexey could communicate with Elisey in town. He was also hunkered down in his own apartment. Rita and Alexey still had electricity and water for a while. Soon, however, those utilities were turned off. They used a water barrel for a few days. They had a landline, too, which still worked so they were able to call Jana and Oksana several times a day and tell them that they were still alive and healthy. Their daughters told them to go to Jana's apartment building, which had a big basement; they changed their hiding place and settled into the basement of Jana's house for the next ten days. Many neighbors and friends joined them in this shelter.

There was constant bombardment outside. It was a difficult, traumatic time, recalled Rita. July turned into August. After ten days, Elisey arrived and told them that in forty minutes they would all leave the basement where they had found shelter and would soon leave the city of Pervomaisk altogether. Forty minutes – that was the timeline for Rita to prepare herself to step into the war-torn outside world. Rita said they had nothing with them. She was wearing a sundress and slippers; she had not packed any clothes. But there was no time to pack anything now; it was simply too dangerous for anyone to go to their own apartments to gather belongings.

Alexey stubbornly declined to leave the basement or seek safety somewhere else. He wanted to stay in this basement and in Pervomaisk. He asked Elisey for some money to make it through the next few days. But Elisey reasoned with him. Rita said she doesn't even remember what they were talking about. She did not interfere at first. Was there even a plan? What was going on outside the building? One thing that became clear was that there was absolutely no city transportation available for any kind of evacuation, absolutely none. Alexey still did not want to leave the city and abandon all their possessions. Rita persuaded him to at least go to Elisey's apartment and make further plans. So, the first stop of their escape route was Elisey's apartment.

As Rita and Alexey arrived, Elisey's parents were arriving, too. Additionally, Alexey's parents also came to Elisey's apartment. It was a large group. Rita remembered rummaging through their valuables, assessing how much money they had. Alexey still wanted to stay and keep the money to survive for a while. Rita finally yelled at him, and Alexey decided that maybe it was best to evacuate, after all.

Using Elisey's car, they all drove to the church to meet the others who would evacuate with them. Everyone there was in a panic. The people were told that within two hours, a cease fire would be in effect, and the convoy could leave. The group had to wait till late into the afternoon. Elisey was organizing cars to drive his church members out of Pervomaisk.

Elisey described the evacuation efforts in this way in his book:[5]

> We continued to inform people, relatives, Christians, friends. We needed drivers. We needed vehicles. There were no communications. It was very hard to gather people together. The brothers were rushing around the city. Of course, any kind of movement around the city was potentially deadly. Any second there could be a bomb explosion. On every road intersection there were gunmen, who had the authority to shoot or grab you...The city was deathly

---

[5] Ibid., 143.

> empty. All cars were being expropriated and taken by terrorists for their own purposes. By the mercies of God … we remained unnoticed and unharmed. We gathered near School #1. We completely packed the vehicles with people. There was no room for anybody to take anything with them. There was nothing more valuable than human life.

Rita recalled that, finally, the convoy was indeed allowed to leave the city while the cease fire took effect. Rita remembered that she was in a black Jeep for this part of her escape. Belongings had to be left behind, as every spare inch was needed to transport people out of the war zone. The convoy drove directly to the Ukrainian territory, never stopping along the way, for it was simply too dangerous. Arriving in safety, she met many of her friends from Pervomaisk. They all exchanged stories of what they had witnessed and experienced. The big question now was: How was life to continue, now that they had left their lives behind and could not return to their home town? The local people helped the refugees in many practical ways, with shelter, food, some clothing.

Many refugees made immediate plans to head to Kyiv. Rita and Alexey wanted to go to Kyiv, too, and so they joined this group, traveling by cars. After this initial evacuation, and knowing his family was safe, Elisey returned to Pervomaisk to help other people evacuate while it was still possible. Rita remembered that she arrived in Kyiv, frightened, sad, feeling the danger still following her. She called her granddaughter Viola, who at this time was still at the Christian camp Word of Life outside of Kyiv with the youth group from Pervomaisk. She told Viola that she and Alexey had arrived with a large group of refugees and they all needed shelter. Rita also called Elisey about their safe arrival in Kyiv.

The immediate difficulty for all the refugees was where to live. Elisey called around and was able to secure a place for Rita and Alexey at Word of Life. This summer camp and Bible institute had been transformed into a refugee camp. Viola, Rita's granddaughter, and her youth group had lived there for several weeks already. Now Rita and Alexey would move there temporarily. They ended up living at the camp for nine months. Rita said the camp was a good situation. They had a room, meals were provided, and they shared a bathroom and a toilet with others on the floor. Life was difficult, but all the people there were in the same situation. Having lost everything, and not being able to go back to their former lives, everyone wondered what the future would look like. They all had experienced trauma and shock, and it took time to regain some balance in life.

News from the conflict zone depressed her. In August 2014, they learned that their Baptist church, the one Alexey had built with his own hands, had been burned to the ground by the separatists. It was sad and traumatic news. Rita was unable to express her feelings; it was just too overwhelming to talk about it.

Their son-in-law, Pastor Elisey, described his emotions about the church burning in his book in this way: "It seemed to us that it just could not be true. The building had such beautiful architecture and a huge, bright sanctuary. The walls were painted with murals, and we had oak flooring; the furniture and sound equipment and the shining cupolas ... did it really all burn down? It just couldn't be true! Yet it was."[6]

After nine months at Word of Life camp, Rita and Alexey rented a small apartment in the spring of 2015 in Brovary, outside Kyiv. She began working again in a beauty salon. They lived there for one and a half years. While living in Brovary, Rita went several times to Kyiv to visit her daughter Jana. She recalled that these visits were characterized by emotional dead weight and stupor. The visits were not enjoyable or memorable because Rita was so extremely homesick for life in Pervomaisk. She longed to go home to her city. Rita experienced loss and grief in all its depths. At night, she would lie down on her bed and feel frozen and stiff. There was no vibrant life left in her. She was looking back to the wonderful, peaceful life they had had in Pervomaisk where they owned a home, were part of a lively, healthy church, had many friends and enjoyed living close to most of their family. It was easy to walk to work through a nearby park. She had enjoyed her work at the salon. All of this was gone – a life left behind – never to be retrieved again.

The depression went to such depth that Rita could not think about or plan a new life. Thinking was simply impossible, she said. It was like there was a great blank sheet with nothing written on it about her future. Even though their current situation in the rented apartment was good, she could not see further than the next moment. She had

---

[6] Ibid., 150.

grocery stores and health clinics in the neighborhood, she had one daughter nearby in Kyiv, and their apartment was warm and comfortable. They were safe and so was most of their family. God had truly provided for her and Alexey in every way, but Rita said, "My life had stopped."

Then Oksana called them. Elisey and Oksana Pronin had by this time spent nine months in the US, had returned to Ukraine, and were living and working in L'viv. They invited Rita and Alexey to move to L'viv. The couple decided that this was the next step on their journey, and in November 2015 they made the move to Western Ukraine. When they arrived, the Pronin's small group numbered about ten to fifteen people, all from Pervomaisk. It was a great reunion. Friends from back home fell into each other's arms, cried and laughed together. It was the beginning of a new life.

Looking back, Rita remembers that her home in Pervomaisk had always been a place of rest, refreshment, community, and safety. Grandkids would play, and adult children would share life with their parents. To be without a home for so long had taken such an emotional toll on Rita, she could hardly describe it.

The first move, to Kyiv, was scary and necessitated by war. In their new location, they had to figure out how and where to get official documents and permits. She was at that time already eligible for retirement benefits, but she did not know what address she should even put on the government forms. Where they were living was temporary; where they would be living, she did not know. They had also applied to the government for humanitarian aid for refugees. Rita recalled that at their age, a forced relocation due to the traumas of war was a huge challenge in every way, physically, emotionally, mentally.

The second move, to L'viv, was by choice. They had the support of family, they could choose a place to rent, and life in L'viv began with encouragement, perspective, and hope. God had been faithful, leading Rita and Alexey on a path they would never have chosen, but on which they learned to trust Him even more and for everything.

Rita and Alexey are now a big part of the new church plant, *Disciples Church*. Their son-in-law is the new pastor, and their daughter Oksana hosts small groups, teaches a Ladies Bible Study, and serves alongside her husband. Rita said now, she would not return to Pervomaisk. She has a new life here, difficult as it was to start over several times. The Word of Life camp in Borispil, the small apartment in Brovary, and now their new apartment in L'viv are markers on her life journey. In all these places, she created a home, a nest, a place of refuge from the storm. She did experience great trauma and went through a deep depression. But now she no longer feels in a stupor. In fact, her ministry at *Disciples Church* is mainly focused on providing practical help to other refugees still arriving in the city. She oversees the humanitarian aid that *Disciples Church* provides and manages the donations coming in from Switzerland and other places. In her free time and just for fun, she cuts and colors hair for friends and family.

CHAPTER FOUR

Viola

Viola was born on May 14th in 2000 in the town of Pervomaisk. Viola's grandpa was the pastor at the local Baptist church, her grandma Rita was his faithful helper as the pastor's wife. Her parents and grandparents were a great example and influence in her life, said Viola. Her dad, Elisey, had been involved in serving at the church as long as she can recall. Before her dad became the senior pastor in 2007, he served as deacon and as youth pastor. Viola's mom, Oksana, always sang in the church choir. Most of Viola's life revolved around the church. Because she saw the clear example of her parents serving in the church, the desire to also serve God in and through the church began early in Viola's life.

Viola had a cat named Simba while growing up. He was a multicolored cat and she loved him dearly. A small puppy kind of belonged to her household, too, but he lived more on the streets of Pervomaisk than at home. This dog, once fully grown, was eventually given to the church, to be a watch dog and protect the church grounds.

During the summer months, Viola enjoyed the camps her church organized for young people. Sometimes it would be a tent camping event, at other times camps would be held at a retreat center. Many young people from all over the region would come to these camps. Viola's summers were completely focused on this ministry of the church. She was able to invite some of her friends from school to these camps. Viola reflected that these were the happiest times of her life.

In Pervomaisk it was possible to just walk down the streets and find kids to play with. From morning to evening, life was lived on the streets of the town. Children would hang out with neighbors and play with other kids, always watched over by a nearby neighbor. The kids would walk and play and run and hide, till they heard someone's mom yell, "Time for dinner!" Walking on the streets was a way of life —for community, for friendships, for learning and sharing.

Viola's favorite subjects in school were always English, then Ukrainian, and then Ukrainian literature. In general, Viola enjoyed subjects like history and language much better than math and physics. The first three years of elementary school she spent in a small public school in the center of Pervomaisk, which was considered prestigious and modern, but was a 20-minute walk from her home. She then transferred to another elementary school, closer to home. Here the children came from poorer families, but she made very good friends there and liked it better than her first school.

One girl became her best friend, and people would say that they were like twins. They would dress alike, would do things in the same way, and would also go to summer camps together. Eventually, they attended youth group together and went to church together. Their friendship started in third grade and lasted till the end of 8th grade, when the war came.

Many students in Pervomaisk took music lessons after school. Viola attended music and art school in the Baptist church. Viola plays the piano, but she is not very confident in her ability. At church, Viola started to work with Olya, who was her Sunday school teacher; Viola helped her with the youngest children in the class. (Olya's story is in chapter four.) This was Viola's first experience of serving God at the local church.

As a young teenager Viola participated in the youth club JAM, Jesus and Me. She belonged to the younger section in JAM, while sisters Lena and Vika, whom you will meet in chapters seven and eight, were in the older youth group. When Viola advanced to the upper class in the youth club, Vika and Lena had already left for university. Viola said all her life circulated around the activities of the church. She was part of a small group for young people and also joined the small group for young women that Ruslana led. (Ruslana's story is in chapter six.) All week long, Viola was busy with ministry-related activities, besides studying at school and taking music and art lessons. Looking back, she said she does not understand now how she had the energy to manage all of this. But she remarked that the town was so small that it was easy to get together with people and do things together.

Viola grew up in a Christian family where her mom and dad constantly served at the church. She was frequently at church, and this was just normal in her childhood. But Viola said she did not recognize how important life with God really was. She thought that coming to church, being at the youth group, fellowshipping before and after the worship service, was simply a great time of hanging out and being with friends. She did not understand that God has a purpose and task for the church, that there is a mission of God for the world, that these friends were more than just buddies, and that people should be invited to church to hear the good news. The best thing that could happen, she thought was for people to come to church, to youth group, and hang out together. She liked the worship music and she liked listening to the sermons.

In the summer of 2014, she was leaving for camp with her youth group. Even though she was only fourteen years old, she began to understand, from the news and conversations around her, that things were changing in her country. The group went to *Word of Life* camp in Kyiv for two weeks. During these two weeks, war broke out in Pervomaisk, and the youth group could not return home.

This was a very hard time for Viola. She struggled with not seeing her family, especially her grandma Rita, with whom she was very close. She did not know what would happen tomorrow, what was God's plan in all of this. Could war possibly come to Kyiv as well? These were real fears for a teenager.

Being separated from all that was familiar, especially friends, family, and her church, was very difficult for Viola. She wanted to see her friends again, she missed her home and her family. Viola said she had to learn to hope in God alone. And she learned that God does not just live far away in heaven--He was really nearby and close to her heart. God helped her during this time to know Him. She learned a lot about who God is and what He had done for her personally. She was beginning to understand that life was meant to be a living relationship with God. So, at the camp in Kyiv she dedicated her life to God.

Viola initially left for summer camp, planning to spend two wonderful weeks there with her youth group. She ended up staying the whole summer as war broke out in her hometown. Viola said that during the initial camp time, she was simply a camper, enjoying the activities. But once it was decided that the group would live there for the unforeseeable future, due to the war, Viola began working and helping at the camp. The youth group boys were working in the forest and the girls helped in the kitchen. Viola remembered that her hands were cut up and sore from peeling many vegetables.

During this time, Viola's family was spread out all over the country. Her mother, Oksana, her brother, David, and one grandma, Tanya, had fled the city of Pervomaisk and lived in a refugee camp in Vinnytsia. In this camp, only women and children found refuge and shelter. Viola was thankful that at least part of her family was safe. They were able to talk by phone regularly, but neither Oksana nor Viola had internet at this time.

Viola's father, Elisey, had remained in Pervomaisk. There, electricity was turned off, so the telephone lines did not work and the internet was disconnected. The family could not communicate with each other. It was an extremely difficult time for Viola. She did not know what was going on in her hometown, if her dad was well and safe, healthy or injured by bombs or shrapnel. Elisey was able to call his wife only one time for two minutes from an old phone. His message was, "I am well. Don't worry. All will be well and normal again." Very irregularly, Elisey would be able to send a text message to Oksana, who would then immediately call Viola with the news. This uncertainty went on all summer; Viola endured spotty communication, had no family nearby; fear and worry for her dad dominated her every thought.

As the end of the summer of 2014 neared, Viola began to think about school. She was supposed to start high school, 9th grade, but the family was still spread out all over Eastern Ukraine. Viola already understood and accepted that a return to Pervomaisk was not a possibility. Of course, somehow the family wanted to live together again; they had not seen each other all summer. Viola's parents made plans to move to the south side of Donetsk, in the Ukrainian territory. The town had formerly been occupied by Russian forces, but had been freed by the Ukrainian army in their offensive push. The family would not be living at home in Pervomaisk, but close by, as Severodonetsk was located just a few miles from the actual front line of the war. A Christian family offered them an apartment to live in. Oksana, who had very mixed feelings about this move, travelled to Kyiv to pick up Viola. The two of them, along with little David, then moved to this apartment in the late summer of 2014, and finally Elisey was also able to join his family in this town.

The family lived in Severodonetsk for four months. The emotional toil of the past few months and the present danger to their lives was huge. Viola said she did not really understand what was going on. She wondered what was happening to her life. As she started high school, Viola lived with danger, great stress, and emotional exhaustion. Her father went back into the conflict zone repeatedly, helping other people. School did not go well. She simply could not grasp what was happening. Ruslana lived with Viola's family during this time also.

Viola recalled some especially stressful situations. Every week, in order to buy groceries, she needed to pass through control points along the border. She was walking home from school one day, and her parents were doing something in another town nearby. Ruslana was home to welcome Viola from school. Suddenly, the alarms and sirens went off everywhere, which could only mean one thing – bombing was about to commence. Everyone on the streets panicked and started running home or to find shelters. All cars disappeared quickly from the streets and Viola ran home as fast as she could.

The family lived on the 7th floor. Viola had the forethought to not take the elevator in case of a power outage. She ran up the stairs in seconds, banging on the door till Ruslana opened it. Ruslana was also in shock about the events unfolding. They looked at each other and realized they were home alone. What should they do? What would they need to do if war returned to this part of the city? Viola's parents were in another town. How could they get in touch with them? Where could they find shelter? What other city was reachable by foot? They were so afraid and anxious. Viola and Ruslana started to call around to friends and church members, but the electricity was unstable and unreliable. Suddenly, an all-clear sound was heard. They found out that this event was a drill for the very real possibility of invasion. Their nerves were at a breaking point.

Often the family would travel to a very small town near Pervomaisk where some shut-in members of their Pervomaisk congregation were living. Many people had found a temporary refuge in these apartments with relatives and friends from the church. Viola's family would bring these families fresh groceries. Viola said that on these trips she came so close to being home that she could see her house, her school, her street. From her outlook, she could even see the ruins of the church her grandpa had built and that her dad had pastored for so many years; the distance to home could have been covered by foot in forty minutes. "You could almost be home - but you couldn't go home." This was very difficult, Viola recalled, a heart-felt trial, and her emotions came out in tears. All you wanted to do was to walk home - and it was not possible.

People were still thinking that maybe after a short time, all the fighting would finally cease and they could return home. The thought that she would never return home never crossed Viola's mind – it was unthinkable.

After four months of living under such stress near the war zone, and considering all the prior months in refugee camps, Viola's parents accepted an invitation by American friends to fly the family to the US and take some time to recover from the turmoil and the trials. So, during the Thanksgiving holiday week of 2014, the family flew to the US and lived in the state of Kansas. A new life started for Viola in America. But living in America meant Viola could not be in close contact with her Ukrainian friends due to the time difference (8 hours from Kansas). That was a great loss.

Viola started high school in Kansas and made new friends during this season of her life. She attended 9th grade for nine months in the US. Viola said she liked America very much. Every day she liked going to school. Being there was almost like a fairy tale for her after the trauma of the previous months. She had friends, she was safe, she could do what she wanted to do, and she tried track and field for the first time. She joined the school choir and sang with her class mates. And she played in the school orchestra. At the local Baptist church she would attend youth group and worship services with her family. And as a family they also had the opportunity to travel around the US a little, so Viola saw Minnesota, Missouri, and other states. Viola recalled seeing films about America in school back in Pervomaisk, but now she was actually living in the US.

Viola said her greatest problem in America was that she really missed her extended family members, like grandparents, cousins, and her friends. She was especially close to her grandma Rita. It was very seldom possible to call these people on the phone, and so Viola cried a lot during these months. Their host, Susan, would comfort Viola with kisses from her grandparents to each cheek. Viola said at the beginning of her time in the US, even though she really liked it, she wanted desperately to go back to Ukraine to be with her family and friends. She told her parents boldly that she was a Ukrainian patriot and did not want to live abroad. "Send me back to Ukraine, please!" was her constant plea. But over time she adjusted well to her new life in America and was less eager and determined to return to Ukraine. Living in the US long term began to sound like a really good plan to her.

But then her parents decided to return to Ukraine. Viola remembered screaming and yelling, "I don't want to leave here. I have a future here in America; I want to stay! You are taking everything away from me again!" But it was no use. Viola could not stay in the States without her parents, and her parents were called to return to Ukraine. So, the family flew back to their homeland late in the summer of 2015. They landed purposefully in the city of L'viv this time, for a new season of ministry and service was about to begin.

Elisey started working at the Ukrainian Baptist Theological Seminary, and also had plans to start a new church. Initially, Viola cried a lot and just wanted to return to America. But again, school started. Viola repeated 9th grade and made new friends, in L'viv this time. Her father started a small church plant, *Disciples Church,* and Viola found herself serving there as much as she could. She especially got involved in the youth ministry of *Disciples Church* and helped in Sunday school. She was baptized in 2016, the first believer to join *Disciples Church* through baptism. She was sixteen years old. She started to feel more comfortable with each passing week in L'viv. She thought, "After all, these are my people, these Ukrainians." She found many opportunities for telling people on the street and in her school about God and a personal relationship with Him.

Viola finished high school in L'viv and, in the fall of 2018, entered the technical university as a student in the field of applied linguistics. She said that she hopes that the way God has led her will be a testimony to others to walk with God and trust Him. She knows L'viv is God's place for her; God led her here, and she is supposed to study and serve here right now. God knows what her future holds, and she trusts Him. Viola learned to follow God one step at a time. When the next step became clear, she took it by faith. She believes nothing happens by chance; it is all God's good plan unfolding. As tough as her experience has been, she is thankful for a faithful God.

Viola never returned home to Pervomaisk. Various people from the church have been able to go to her house there and collect some of her clothes and personal belongings and sent these to Viola when they were outside the occupied territory again. Viola said so far, she has had three lives: her first one was in Pervomaisk, her second one was for a brief time in the US, and now she is enjoying her third life in L'viv. And she laughed and said, "I am only eighteen. We'll see what else will happen with my life." Each of these lives has been completely different from the others.

Some people from her old life, like Olya, Anton, and Ruslana, have reappeared in her new third life, as they have also moved out of the war zone and resettled in L'viv. Her friend from 3rd grade has reconnected recently with Viola. Due to the war, they had not seen each other for four years. They were able to communicate with letters and emails as her friend had moved with her family to Poltava. In the summer of 2018, Viola was able to finally meet up with her friend in Kyiv, where her friend studies now. It was a wonderful reunion.

Viola has developed a radically different worldview through these experiences. Her understanding has completely changed; she sees people, God, and all circumstances in a new light. Viola rests in God's sovereignty. She still has nightmares and flashbacks to the traumatic experiences she lived through. Often images of Pervomaisk go through her troubled dreams; the destruction of her home church by separatist arsonists is still painful in her mind. These nightmares are accompanied by sweating and a racing heartbeat. But she turns to God for comfort and gives Him her cares because she knows now that He is faithful.

CHAPTER FIVE

Olya

Olya was born October 14, 1986. She grew up in Pervomaisk, in the Lugansk region of Ukraine. Her parents, Galina and Sasha, have been the most influential people in her life. She had two grandmothers who she was close to, and she spent lots of time visiting the grandma who lived in Pervomaisk. Olya had a cat for a while, but it was stolen. Her summers were spent at different summer camps.

Olya did not like to go to school, mainly because the staff and students would make fun of her because she came from a Baptist family. The town was small, and everyone knew everyone's business. After graduation, she studied law, because her dad had some legal problems in his work and decided, "We need a lawyer in the family." Her university was in Lugansk, about an hour's drive from Pervomaisk.

Olya's studies were organized in modules, so she would attend lectures at the university four times a year. In between these lectures, Olya would work and gain experience in the corporate world. Her first job was working in a hospital as a secretary. She liked it a lot, but when she graduated from the university, God gave her a new job, a real dream job, as an assistant notary. She gained a lot of life and work experience there. She worked about five years in this job, till the summer of 2014 when everything in her life changed.

Olya's mom, Galina, had repented when Olya was ten years old. Since then, mom and grandma took Olya to the church in Pervomaisk at every opportunity. It was a traditional Baptist Church. Olya, a young teenager, did not like it very much. Three preachers every Sunday shared sermons that young people could not understand. Olya didn't have friends at church, either, so she really didn't want to go to the worship services. But her mom insisted that she go every Sunday.

Galina also attended all other services during the week and dragged Olya with her. The church had services on Wednesday, Saturday evening, Sunday morning, and Sunday evening. Olya decided one day not to go to all the services. She informed her mom that she would only attend Sunday evening. Her mom looked at her and informed her that as long as she lived at home, she would do as she was told, and she would go every time there was a worship service. Olya was very upset, crying about this apparent injustice and the demands of her mom.

But eventually, she began to like church more. She made a lot of friends at church and started to visit Sunday school on Sunday morning. Oksana Pronin was her first Sunday school teacher, and Olya liked her very much right away.

The church did not have an official youth group at this time; there was only Sunday school for all ages with a youth leader for the older teenagers. Youth group participants had to be eighteen years old or older. But Olya and some of her girlfriends from church wanted to be part of some youth group events. They asked the youth leader if he would make an exception and allow them to attend the youth meetings in a neighboring town with the youth group from church. They were allowed to participate and travel with the youth group to a nearby city.

A speaker from America addressed the youth rally and shared the gospel simply and plainly. That day Olya and several other teens from the church repented. Olya became a believer at the age of thirteen, and publicly confessed her faith in Jesus Christ. Her church's policy was that a person must be sixteen years old to be baptized. The annual baptismal service was held in the summer. Olya's birthday wasn't till October, though, so she had to wait till the following summer to be baptized, which really distressed her.

Olya began serving in the church, and the church became her life. She was involved in many ministries over the years in Pervomaisk Baptist Church. She helped in the kids' ministry, taught Sunday school, and eventually became the director of the Sunday school. She also helped at the numerous summer camps. She served in the music ministry, playing the piano for the choir and playing in the praise band, as well.

As this praise group was formed, other girls joined in, and they all became very good friends. They played six or seven years together, wrote their own songs, performed in some weddings and events in the region, and gained a reputation for being an excellent band in eastern Ukraine.

Olya had followed the news out of Kyiv in 2013 about the protests and the unrest. She knew that Crimea had been annexed by Russia by early 2014. Olya recalled that very strange things were beginning to happen in her city. Her pastor, Elisey Pronin, described the unfolding threat in his book:

After the congress, we all felt the wave of separatism sweep through our eastern cities: Donetsk, Lugansk, Odessa, Kharkov, and Slavyansk. Agitators showed up everywhere, held meetings; Ukrainian flags were lowered and removed, Russian flags were raised instead. Heavily armed people showed up from seemingly nowhere, started taking over local administrations and offices.[7]

Olya remembered that powerful people called Elisey and asked him to support the separatist movement, but he refused to align himself with these self-appointed "authorities". As a result, Elisey received threats against his life and ministry. He was told that he would face dire consequences if he would not support the Lugansk People's Republic. The separatists threatened to harm Elisey's family and burn the church. Elisey shared these terrifying messages with his church family. Everyone was very frightened to hear the threats, Olya said. All the brothers and deacons gathered and started to pray hard. They called the police to ask for protection, but the police didn't want to help the church in any way. The brothers decided to keep watch over the church building themselves.

Soldiers appeared in another city, about 100 km from Pervomaisk. One former church member, who had moved to this city, called the brethren and described the terrible events going on. The whole church family felt bad and worried about the events far away, but no one expected in the least that this unrest would reach Pervomaisk. Olya and her mom went to church, prayed for protection, and joined in night prayer watches. God protected this group of believers for a long time, Olya said.

The so call 'democratic referendums' were held in the Donetsk and Lugansk regions on May 11, 2014, to legitimize the establishment of the self-declared republics. The results of these separatist referendums

---

[7] Ibid., 77.

were not recognized by any government. The referendums were considered illegal, unconstitutional, and lacking legitimacy. Olya and her folks in Pervomaisk were told that the referendum would be officially binding for the region and the city. In May 2014, the Lugansk referendum passed.

Olya reflected that after the declaration of the Lugansk People Republic, LPR, they continued for a while to live a somewhat stable life in Pervomaisk. The church family prayed a lot together. Crimea had been annexed, Lugansk and Donetsk were now independent republics. At this point, very few men in uniform could be seen on the streets of Pervomaisk. The people did not yet realize that the soldiers and mercenaries were in hiding, waiting for the appointed time to take over the city. Olya described it as the silence before the storm.

Olya and her mom had made vacation plans for the summer of 2014, to spend some relaxing time at the beach. The church still had plans for some summer camps. The church also sent the youth group to Kyiv, to *Word of Life,* as planned. The current situation was tense, but Olya and Galina decided to get away for two weeks from all the tension of the area. Their original vacation spot had been in Crimea, which was now not accessible due to the annexation. They were planning to travel by train to another place on the Black Sea that was still part of Ukraine. They had an invitation from friends, so it was a cheap getaway. They packed lightly, summer clothes for two weeks, most certainly expecting to return home after some rest and sunshine.

Thinking that their documents might come in handy, they packed their passports, some other documents, and some extra money in their suitcases. The first week of their vacation was fine; Olya and Galina enjoyed the beach and the sea. But then Olya's employer called and told her not to come back to the city of Pervomaisk, because the fighting was coming closer to the city every day. Mom and daughter decided to stay put for the near future, but were worried about the events unfolding in Pervomaisk.

Olya followed the news on TV and the internet, anxious about her family, friends, and her home. On one news clip, she actually saw their apartment building on TV, and it was on fire. "I saw my windows," Olya said. People posted pictures on Facebook of her building, flames flickering through the windows. Later postings confirmed that the fire had been put out and her apartment was safe. It was a miracle that her building survived the fire. Many family members had stayed in that building because it had a good basement that offered protection.

Her city was eventually bombed and shelled by rebel forces. Pervomaisk found itself in the middle of the conflict zone in the summer of 2014. People were hiding in her building, seeking shelter from shrapnel. One bomb hit the garden in which Olya had played.

The church started to organize car convoys to evacuate people as soon as a cease fire would hold. From far away, Olya tracked all the events taking place in her home town. It was unbelievable to her. The rebel forces would allow only a few hours for an evacuation; people would leave the city by car, on foot, on bicycles, by any means possible, just to get out.

Olya's dad was still in Pervomaisk. Galina and Olya called him and begged him to leave; the situation was very dangerous and worsening. He told them that everything was still okay, not to be afraid for him, that he was fine, but his voice was very distraught, Olya remembered with tears.

Olya's father did not want to leave during the evacuation window, because he still believed that the conflict would be over soon. He thought the Ukrainian army would restore peace and order to the region, and Pervomaisk would be free again. Many people like her dad were expecting the green army to arrive in town. That's what they were told to expect by local news. Everyone wanted to believe this scenario; no one wanted to leave home. But the situation got worse and worse, Olya remembered, and she was processing it all from her distant observation spot. Sometimes she was able to call and reach her dad, sometimes not. Olya and her mom continued to pressure her dad to please leave the city. But her dad stayed on.

By now, Olya and her mom needed to make some arrangements to stay long-term in their current place or relocate to another city. They were running out of money, but they did not know where to go next. Going home was not an option. A friend offered them his apartment in Kyiv for a couple of months while he and his family were spending some time in the country. They received the apartment keys and took a train to Kyiv in August 2014.

The looming, ever-present, overarching question was still what to do next. They lived in Kyiv for an unforeseeable time. Friends gave them some money to live on. Olya was still hoping to return home to Pervomaisk after a month in Kyiv, but one month turned into two months, then three. And instead of their returning to their hometown, they saw more people arriving in Kyiv from Pervomaisk, seeking shelter as refugees.

Olya and her mom had a pastor friend in the city. This man decided that his church was going to help the refugees, so Olya and Galina moved to the premises of the church for temporary living. The church used their Sunday school class rooms for bedrooms. Showers and toilets were available, and there was no cost to the refugees for shelter and food.

In Pervomaisk, there was no end in sight to the fighting and the bombing. Olya's dad finally left the city, too. He took his bike and cycled ten miles on back roads into Ukrainian territory to a nearby refugee camp run and supported by the Baptist church of Pervomaisk. The camp volunteers helped Olya's dad to get to Kyiv to join Olya and her mom at the church shelter. Trains were no longer running to and from Kiev, so they found a bus for Sasha instead.

The refugees at camp still expected to eventually head back home, but the leaders cautioned the people that a return would be unlikely. The atmosphere was grim. Many members of Olya's home church in Pervomaisk worked at the refugee camps near the beleaguered city. They stayed, even though they were afraid, and served the masses of refugees pouring into the Ukrainian territory.

It was hard to get honest, accurate news from the conflict zone, Olya remembered. Some people at the Kyiv church building still had relatives living in the war zone. They got more current and objective news, but with difficulty. Olya and Galina constantly thought about what to do next, where to move to next. Olya had other relatives living in more distant areas of Ukraine, but no one invited her and her mom to come live with them. "We also had relatives in the region, but they didn't even ask us if we were alive and well or what had happened. They did not invite us; these relatives didn't even call." It was a sobering, sad reality.

In contrast, their spiritual family, their brothers and sisters in Christ, supported and encouraged them. The church building became home to about thirty-five people. They functioned like one big family, used one kitchen, shared one refrigerator. It was a good time, recalled Olya, despite the immediate challenging circumstances. Emotions were high, of course, and Olya remembered crying and praying together. Olya said everyone would constantly think of what was going on at home. They all wondered what to do next and where to go from here.

Olya had already obtained a US visa in her passport. She worked with American teams for summer camps in Pervomaisk and had been invited to visit America many times. Her American friends, Susan and

Dan, lived in Kansas. They called Olya on Skype often during this time to find out what was going on, what had really happened, and they invited her to go to America for some rest.

In November 2014, Olya decided to go to the States for a while, to rest and regain some emotional and physical balance. Friends helped her with buying the tickets and getting her on the way. Her parents were in favor of this recreation time for her. It was a very stressful time for everyone.

Olya planned to be in the US from November 2014 till January 2015. She spent Christmas in America, a dream she had had for a long time. Olya's host family was very kind and helpful. Olya said it was such a contrast of life between war-torn Ukraine and the peaceful state of Kansas. She was still stressed about the events at home, but having distance between her and the awful situation helped, especially since she knew that her parents were safe. Her time went by quickly, and she had return tickets to Kyiv; but her hosts encouraged her to change her flights and stay longer in the US. They were also suggesting options for Olya's future, one being to stay and work in the US.

Olya prayed about extending her stay and decided to remain in the US for a few more months. She was able to travel some during her time in America. She visited Ukrainian friends who had immigrated with their families to Portland, Oregon. Another dream came true on this trip, as she had longed to see the Pacific Ocean. Olya was also invited to a wedding and traveled to Florida with Susan and Dan. Olya experienced Florida in all its fullness, with Disney World and beaches and sunshine. Olya's summer destination in 2015 was Colorado, another dream for her. Susan's daughter needed a babysitter and hired Olya for the job. Olya spent ten months in the US, but she missed her home and family and friends. She longed to go home. But where was home now?

"I made the decision to return to Ukraine; it was my homeland, after all," said Olya. She announced her decision to the local church she had attended with Susan and Dan. Olya arrived back in Kyiv at the end of August 2015.

Pastor Elisey had already moved his family to L'viv and had started to work at UBTS. He called Olya and invited her to L'viv to see if she could imagine living there and working at UBTS, too. Olya laughed at this suggestion, but told Elisey she would come out to L'viv, just to see the city and the Pronin family again.

She had begun to look for work in Kyiv, but had found nothing that she felt good about, and she had not made any work commitments. As plans were made for the L'viv visit, Elisey called her again, telling her that she had an interview on Tuesday with Slavik Pyzh, president of UBTS. Olya bought her train tickets, went to L'viv, interviewed with Slavik and received a job offer. She was to work in the academic office of UBTS, starting as soon as possible since the new academic year was about to begin. Back in Kyiv, she told her parents that she had accepted a job in L'viv. She began working at UBTS at the end of September 2015.

Moving was not complicated, as she had no personal belongings except some suitcases. Initially, she lived with friends in the city while looking for a rental place. It was hard to find a decent, inexpensive flat, but Olya eventually found a nice little place and moved into it. She began a new life at the end of October 2015, establishing a home again, this time in L'viv.

Within a year, Olya invited her parents to move to L'viv and live with her. Galina and her husband were reluctant to leave Kyiv, because they had found a new church family and work. The pastor did not want to lose them as members of his congregation either.

Exciting things were happening in Olya's family at this time. Her dad had accepted Christ and become a Christian in Kyiv during this time of forced relocation amid the turmoil of war. Back in Pervomaisk, he very seldom had gone to church. Now, as a refugee living in a church building, Olya's dad was surrounded by God's love and God's people 24/7. He saw true Christian faith lived out daily. The church became his family and small group his home, and he drew closer to God.

Olya closed her interview with some reflections. She has no relatives living in Pervomaisk anymore. One uncle, who had stayed behind, died recently. She still knows of older folks who live there, who never had the desire to leave their home, no matter who reigned in city hall. They accepted the occupation as a necessary evil, but they don't live in freedom now. Olya's friends have all left – some moved to Poland or America, some to other parts of the world. She has no reason to call anyone in Pervomaisk anymore; she has left her life there behind.

Olya never went back to her home, never saw her house again, never picked up any personal belongings from her apartment. What started as a vacation at the seaside, became a one-way-ticket journey. Olya admitted that she does not keep up with news of the war zone;

the occupied territories are part of her past, but not part of her future. She knows that it is still dangerous there. Olya and her parents still live together in a one-room apartment in L'viv. She enjoys her work at UBTS and rejoices that God has blessed her with work at a Christian institution.

Olya is also an integral part of the new church plant, *Disciples Church,* and Elisey is again her pastor. She serves in the music ministry of the new church, leading the worship team. Her new life includes many new friends and even travel abroad, now that Ukrainians, since July 2017, have been granted free visa travel to certain countries. She said she understands now that material things are not very important in life; we can live without all the stuff, but we cannot live without God and His care.

CHAPTER SIX
Galina

Galina was born in 1958 and grew up in the Donetsk region located in eastern Ukraine. Her father came from Ukraine, but her mother was Russian. She grew up with her older brother in her family's large apartment. Although she did not know her grandparents well because they lived far away, she knew and loved her immediate family, and admired her parents. Her mother worked as a nurse.

After finishing school, Galina studied at the university. During this time, she met her future husband, Sasha. They were studying the same major, electrical engineering. Right after finishing college, Galina and Sasha married and they moved to Pervomaisk in 1985 and began their life together, working, and planning for a family.

Galina did not work long after getting married. Soon they found out that they were expecting their first child. Olya, their little blessing, was born in 1986. She remained their only child. Olya was a sickly child, and Galina stayed home with her and took care of all her needs. She enjoyed being a homemaker, knowing and greeting her neighbors, keeping her home clean and organized. Once Olya became older, her health improved and she started school, so Galina started part-time work.

Galina had married into a Baptist family. Her in-laws were believers, although her husband was not. Sasha knew about God, but he lived like he wanted. No one in Galina's family had been Baptists, but when her mother-in-law invited her to church, she gladly went and soon began attending regularly. Sitting in the beautiful worship services and listening to the word of God, convinced Galina of God's truth and her need for salvation. She made a profession of faith in Christ, but her husband Sasha would wait for a long time to declare his faith in Jesus

Christ. Olya was ten years old when Galina became a Christian. Galina's salvation changed the way she parented. Olya accepted Christ three years later, also at the Baptist church in Pervomaisk.

Galina spent much of her time serving at the church in a variety of ministries. For twenty years she led the prayer group; every morning they met for prayer. She also sang in the choir. Some of her relatives were members of the Baptist church in Pervomaisk. Alexey, Rita's husband, and Sasha were cousins. The name Kiyan was well known in town. They lived near each other and would often meet and serve together at various church events. Their lives were intermingled, and they liked it this way – small town, deep relationships, Galina said. The years went on and life in small town Ukraine was nice. But then the revolution changed her life forever.

In July 2014, Galina understood that the conflict was coming closer and closer to Pervomaisk. She had followed the developing news out of Kyiv and the news of the annexation of Crimea. Her prayer group responded to the ripples of war with prayer meetings at the church every morning. Though the situation was stressful and frightening, the church still sent the youth group to camp in Kyiv. With her daughter Olya, Galina decided to leave town for a while, head to the vacation town of Feodosia in Crimea and wait out the events. Sasha did not want to leave the city; he wanted to stay home and protect the family's personal belongings. But after vacationing for two weeks, it became clear that Galina and Olya could not return home.

Robbers and gangsters had taken over the streets of Pervomaisk; crime was the law; war was the sound track. Bombs were destroying buildings and killing people; shrapnel injured many others. Friends and families were seeking shelter in the basement of buildings, desperate for their lives. Galina marveled that God had protected them from the direct experience of war, as they had left Pervomaisk before the occupiers came.

She and Olya spent a month or so in Feodosia and got their war news through the internet. No one could relax or think about anything but the war. The bad news just kept pouring in. Their apartment building in Pervomaisk was on fire at one point, and they found out through Facebook posts when the fire was finally under control. Criminals roamed the streets and acted authoritatively. Their church and pastor were threatened. Then their beloved church was burned. This happened in August 2014. How much worse could it get? An anticipated cease fire was supposed to enable some people to leave

Pervomaisk, but would it come, and would it hold? Was it more dangerous to leave or to stay?

"God kept my heart quiet," Galina explained. She doesn't quite understand how that could be since her family and her husband were still in occupied Pervomaisk, but she was calm. What happened was indeed horrible, she said, but in her innermost spiritual being, she experienced peace. God supported her nerves and strengthened her hands, helping her to endure this tense and difficult situation.

The general expectation was still that within two to three weeks the conflict and the fighting would be over, and the population could return to their homes. But after Galina had lived in Feodosia for a month, it became clear that the war was not going to end, she said sadly. The troubling questions were: What to do? Where to go? How to live?

A Christian brother called them in Feodosia and offered them his apartment in Kyiv to use as a temporary residence. What a blessing from God this offer was! Galina moved in August 2014 to Kyiv with daughter Olya. They received more help from these Christians: financial aid, clothing and humanitarian items and also fresh produce for their refrigerator. It was an amazing experience of the family of God coming together and meeting dire needs. With tears, Galina recalled that they had no winter clothes by late September, and the pleasant fall weather would soon change to winter bitterness. They had left everything behind in their apartment in Pervomaisk. Their lives were left behind in the East. She experienced such rolling emotions at this time, Galina said.

Galina lived in different places in Kyiv from August 2014 till October 2016. The government helped with some of the needs of the refugees in Kyiv. They were provided with warm winter clothes, coats, and boots. Coupons were given out, allowing the people to get shoes and other clothes. Galina and Olya registered as refugees and were part of this immediate-help program. After a few months in the apartment in Kyiv, the owners returned from their vacation and needed their own home again. A pastoral friend called them just in time and offered them a place in his church building, which was refurnished for refugee use. Galina and Olya relocated to live in this Baptist church in Kyiv for the foreseeable future. More than thirty people lived there together, using Sunday school classrooms as bedrooms.

Sasha was finally able and willing to leave Pervomaisk as well, having experienced the war firsthand for months. Sasha rode his bicycle to get out of Pervomaisk to the nearest refugee camp. Then the church brothers helped him get a ticket for a bus, as no more trains were commuting between the war zone and the capital. Sasha arrived in Kyiv without any personal belongings, because it was simply too dangerous to return to one's apartment since rebel forces had taken over many houses in Pervomaisk.

Galina's brother still lives in the occupied territories with his family. She keeps praying and sharing with them about a new life, not just in L'viv, but a new life in Christ. She has seen some hopeful changes in her brother's life and she continues to pray.

Galina, Olya, and Sasha had lived in Kyiv for about a year when Olya was invited to go to America to get away from the chaotic life in Ukraine. She spent ten months in America, from November 2014 till August 2015, and then came back to join her parents in Kyiv.

Much help was given to Sasha and Galina in their new life situation. They really liked living in Kyiv, Galina said. People were friendly and supportive. There was an abundance of clothing and produce; no one suffered from lack. At the church in Kyiv, Galina and Sasha slept on mattresses on the floor of a children's Sunday School room. Every Sunday, they would need to put their few personal belongings away, because the room would be used for Sunday school, of course. As crazy as this time was, Galina laughed and said it was still a great time. It was an adventure with God. They felt very blessed with all the goodness and kindness the family of God showed them. In the end, Galina and Sasha lived at the church building for almost two years, till October 2016.

Not long after Olya returned from the States, she went to L'viv and, after an interview, received a job offer from Ukrainian Baptist Theological Seminary, Galina reminisced. Olya soon moved to L'viv, but it took her a while to find a nice, affordable apartment to rent. Eventually, Olya was able to invite her parents to move to L'viv to live with her. They relocated to L'viv in the fall of 2016. God still had some amazing plans for this family.

Galina said that once they arrived and settled in, she analyzed their new situation and came to the conclusion that their lives now were better than before the war. God had blessed them in so many ways, with financial support, with humanitarian aid goods, and with a beautiful new city to explore. Galina also had all the necessary documents gathered to retire with a pension from the government. Galina remarked that she really likes her new life here in L'viv.

One huge component of these blessings is that now they go to church together as a family. Back in Pervomaisk, Sasha would not go to church with them. He became a Christian in Kyiv during this time of forced relocation and war turmoil. While he lived as a refugee in a church building, he was surrounded by God's love and God's people. He went to all the small groups that were a part of the church's ministry. When he trusted Christ as his personal Lord and Savior, Galina rejoiced. Once they moved to L'viv, Sasha followed his public confession with believer's baptism at *Disciples Church*. Now, at home, they pray together every evening – something unimaginable before, Galina said. Sasha also found work in L'viv, since, as his wife playfully tells him, he is far from retirement!

With her friend Rita, Galina now manages the work with refugees for *Disciples Church*. She handles the humanitarian aid supplies coming in and going out to needy families and individuals. She is able with a grateful heart to sympathize and help others coming in as refugees. She has received so much help and encouragement that now she gladly shares with all who need it. She loves the new church plant under her pastor Elisey. She is truly happy.

CHAPTER SEVEN

Ruslana

Ruslana was born in Pervomaisk in the Lugansk region in 1993. She is number four among five children, as she has two sisters and two brothers. Her mom was the most influential person in her life. They were very close. Her mom was a homemaker, managing the household and caring for the kids. She showed Ruslana how to live the Christian life and was a good example for her. Ruslana's parents were also very hospitable and had many guests in their home. Their many dogs, cats and parrots were also considered members of the family. In school, Ruslana liked physical education best and math least. She participated in school competitions for sporting events and she dreamed of sport tourism as a future career.

During the summers, she would go to the lake with her friends and do family vacations by the Azov Sea. She would also go with her siblings to visit their grandma and help her, working the potato fields, typical Ukrainian pastime. Oftentimes, she would simply play in the streets of Pervomaisk with other kids, running around, and inventing their own games and schemes. Kids would play a lot on the streets for the simple reason that there were never a lot of toys, and certainly no board games. Ruslana really liked sports as she grew up, and whatever sport she was playing at the moment – soccer, volleyball, baseball – was her favorite! She learned UNO and Chess, though.

Her parents took her to church when she was little, and she was there often. In the summers, Ruslana went to Christian camps. Ruslana said that her parents' influence and testimony was winning her over to a life of faith and belief in Jesus. She always believed in God, she recalled. She saw her need for a personal relationship with God and became a Christian in 2005 at the age of twelve. Her parents were very happy about her personal decision to follow Jesus. But Ruslana waited to be baptized till 2009, as the Baptist church would not baptize people under the age of sixteen. As she became a teenager, she attended youth retreats and camps. She eventually became a leader in these summer camps, working with children and youth.

After finishing high school in Pervomaisk, Ruslana began her studies at Kyiv Theological Seminary (KTS). She pursued these studies in youth ministry for three years, from 2010-2013. It was a non-residential program, so the students would come in for module classes every two or three months, living on campus for a week of classes. Due to the outbreak of war, she was not able to finish her degree there. She also pursued some training in Pervomaisk as a hair stylist, but could not finish it, either, as the outbreak of war interrupted every aspect of life.

After each study period at KTS, Ruslana said she came home with new encouragement and passion and vision for ministry. Her desire to serve God grew ever more. She had the opportunity to serve in the youth group of the church, and also in the youth club JAM, (Jesus And Me). Ruslana became a leader in JAM. Almost every evening there were church-centered activities in Pervomaisk. Ruslana was part of the young adults group and she sang in the choir.

As a teenager, Ruslana had cleaned houses and babysat to earn money. Eventually, she and her sister started their own business. It was a greenhouse business growing and selling fresh vegetables. She became creative in her customer support and delivered her goods to local grocery stores. They had developed business plans and dreamed of extending their acreage, planting more vegetables and building more greenhouses. But the war put an end to all these plans as well.

She met her future husband Anton for the first time at a summer camp in 2010. At the time, she was sixteen years old and Anton was twenty-nine years old. Anton was not yet a believer in Jesus Christ, but God was working in his heart and in his life. When camp was over, Anton left and enrolled in a drug rehabilitation program in a city far away, and Ruslana went back to being a business woman. They did not see each other for four years.

Anton completed rehab and became a Christian. God changed his heart completely and called him into ministry. Anton came back to Pervomaisk and joined the church, working with Elisey Pronin. Ruslana and Anton's friendship blossomed into love, and over time they planned to get married. Anton was then serving in the rehabilitation center, a ministry of the church, where he had come to faith in Christ. In anticipation of a future ministry together, Anton had bought some land near the rehabilitation center so that he and Ruslana could live and work nearby, he in the center, she in her greenhouse business. They had many plans and were anticipating the future as any young happy couple in love would do.

On July 16, 2014, Ruslana was at the last service in the church in Pervomaisk. Very few people attended this service, she remembered, because many people had already left the town due to the increasing danger all around. The news about the war had been getting worse and worse. During this church service, bombs fell on houses in the city, and the house of Ruslana's neighbor experienced a direct hit. They found out about the bomb damage after the service.

On Monday, July 17, 2014, Ruslana's grandmother moved into the home Ruslana shared with her parents and siblings. This grandma had lived in a neighboring city where the bombing already was in full force. Ruslana had planned to go to work for a family that day, doing house cleaning. As she approached this family's house, she found out that soldiers had simply annexed the family's car without any reason or any legal authority.

Ruslana remembered that on that Monday, airplanes came flying very low over the city of Pervomaisk, and the soldiers on the streets started shooting into the sky, aiming for the planes. People who were simply out walking the streets and sidewalks of the city started running as the soldiers opened fire at the planes. No one knew what was going on, or who was shooting at whom.

The circling airplanes were the Ukrainian army, but the city of Pervomaisk was already occupied. How did this happen? The citizens of Pervomaisk had not realized that their city was occupied, because the soldiers hid themselves in homes and stores. But when the airplanes arrived and scanned the situation on the ground, the occupiers came out of their holes like a horde of ants and were suddenly everywhere, Ruslana said, shuddering from the memory.

People started to hide in their apartments, and fear gripped everyone like ice, Ruslana said. She hid in the basement of their house, together with her parents and her grandma. There was no cooking that day – no one was hungry; they only heated water for tea. She did not realize what was happening outside nor the extent of the damage. Later, she realized that this day was the beginning of a war which would force her away from her hometown forever.

During this first week of the war, it was dangerous to walk on the streets. Few people ventured out. Most were hiding, afraid for their lives. Ruslana went out once to buy food. On her way home to the safety of her parents' house, two soldiers stopped her and interrogated her. They wanted to help her carry the bags of food, but Ruslana was so scared that she simply ran away from them to the safety of her shelter. Her grandmother was very frightened during these days, and even refused to go down into the basement. It took a lot of convincing to get her grandma into the cellar for protection from air raids and bombs, Ruslana remembered.

On Tuesday, July 18th, Ruslana's father said that the family should leave the city, but that he would stay behind to protect their property. Ruslana did not want to go and leave her dad behind by himself. She admitted in the interview that she can be very strong-willed, and she did wind up staying with her dad, while her mother and grandma left the city in an evacuation convey. Ruslana's older sister had left the city a week before the war broke out, visiting relatives in another part of Ukraine. Her younger brother had left two weeks earlier for a Christian summer camp in Kyiv, called *Word of Life*. Ruslana's older brother was married and lived with his wife in another city of Ukraine, away from the war zone. And her other sister had already moved to Poland with her husband. So, they were all safe and accounted for. That was a great blessing, Ruslana said.

When the war had started in another town, Slovyansk, everyone had thought, "Oh, Pervomaisk is so small and insignificant; war will not come to us." People were expecting that the war would be over in two days. Bombing started in neighboring cities, but the Ukrainian army moved in and freed those cities. "The same thing will happen in Pervomaisk, too," Ruslana and her dad thought and so they stayed. They barricaded themselves at home, and when the bombs fell, they were hiding in the basement. When the bombing would stop for a while, they would sneak up to look at the damage and return to their apartment with great anxiety. This went on for a whole week. Once, when Ruslana went outside, the impact of a bomb pushed her back into the wall. Her dad felt terribly responsible for the danger she was in, and he cried out, saying, "Why did I not make you leave?!"

On the third day of the bombing, Ruslana remembered waking up at 6 am, very early. The bombing began in all earnest, so Ruslana and her dad ran to the basement and spent the entire day there. It was a very dangerous day. Sometimes Ruslana could discern the noise of a bomb being dropped, and they waited for the impact. Would it be their house this time? Would they ever climb out of their cellar alive and well?

In the basement, conditions deteriorated. It was extremely hot, humid, and dark; across the city there was no electricity, water, or internet. Cell phone services were not working anymore. They couldn't read any news, call any friends, or find out what was going on in the outside world. They were sitting in darkness literally and figuratively. At one point, the occupiers agreed to a cease fire for several hours so that people who wanted to evacuate could leave the city. The notice of the cease fire came at 6:00 a.m. The evacuation was planned for 10:00 a.m. This was the day that Ruslana and her dad decided to leave Pervomaisk. They packed up some of their documents and some clothes, just what they could carry, grabbed their laptop, and, with their neighbors, evacuated the city by car.

All during this week of bombardment, Ruslana had not known where Anton was or if he was even still alive. They had no way of staying in touch, as neither internet nor cell phones were working. One thing Ruslana had heard was that one bomb had landed on the rehabilitation center, but no news about Anton's whereabouts were available. She was emotionally torn up.

A huge convoy of people left the city that day, Ruslana and her dad among them. The evacuees met at the city center. There was only one road cleared to drive out of Pervomaisk; all other roads were blocked or bombed out. Ruslana did not want to leave the city without finding out about Anton. Was he alive, or dead, or injured? But her dad would not let her stay and insisted that she had to leave with him – right then, right now.

Ruslana's dad actually took the lead and drove his car out of town first, followed by everyone who would and could leave Pervomaisk that day. The tragic irony of this day was that even though many people brought suitcases with them to the city center to be part of the evacuation transport, there was no room in the few cars to fit their belongings. It was simply more important to take people out than personal belongings. People had expected buses to be ready for the evacuation, provided by either the Ukrainian government or the occupying forces. But there were no buses. People simply had to ask those with cars if they had room for them, and the belongings had to be left behind. The people were leaving their lives behind. And time was ticking – the cease fire would soon end and the bombing would resume.

Anton did finally manage a call to Ruslana during the evacuation – he was alive, and uninjured. Just hearing his voice calmed Ruslana down in the panicked atmosphere of the moment. But they could not get to him and he could not get to them. He was going to stay behind and help with the evacuation of more people from Pervomaisk and the surrounding cities. Ruslana said a supernatural calm overcame her, and she realized that even though her life was falling apart literally all around her, with God she was safe and secure.

Once the convoy got under way, the road conditions were terrible and it was dangerous to drive on the bombed-out streets. Their flight from the city was miraculous, Ruslana said, because they experienced no air raids or attacks on their way to the first city of refuge. Many people expressed astonishment and wonder that the convoy had arrived safely. Being protected and reaching safety unharmed was a true miracle.

The evacuees kept traveling onward, not really knowing where they were going. No one knew where they would spend the night, where the next meal would come from. One Christian family found out that there was a refugee camp in the city Sumy and told Ruslana and her dad about it. Father and daughter traveled there together, reached the camp, and lived there for the next two to three weeks. This was the initial evacuation phase.

Everyone was still expecting that after several weeks, a return home would be possible. But there would be no return; that became clear very soon, said Ruslana. Incidentally, after she and her dad left their home and their basement shelter, a bomb did hit their yard, and the basement was greatly damaged. Ruslana sees God's complete protection over her life and is grateful her dad was also safe and had evacuated with her.

After she left Pervomaisk, and after living temporarily at the camp in Sumy, Ruslana moved to and lived in a refugee center in Poltava, where she spent her most horrible birthday ever, she said. By now it was August 2014. In the meantime, her mom had arrived in a village near Kyiv. There, inquiring at the city hall about help for refugees, her mom was told that there was a house available from the mayor, which she could manage and occupy with her family. This became the family's new residence, and Ruslana and her dad soon joined her mom there.

Then one day Anton called her and told her he was near Pervomaisk in a town called Severodonetsk. He wanted Ruslana to come to him so they could get married while still on the run as refugees. Anton was helping Elisey Pronin with evacuating more and more people out of Pervomaisk and the surrounding cities. Ruslana's parents were initially not in agreement about these wedding plans. They advised Anton and Ruslana to wait till the war was over. So Ruslana had to keep any further plans a secret from her parents. Including her sister in a 'wedding conspiracy', she bought train tickets to join Anton in Severodonetsk.

But in the end, Ruslana did tell her mom that she was leaving to get married. Her mom resigned herself to the fact of young love and only stipulated that Ruslana must come back to the Kyiv region where the family was now living. Ruslana arrived on Sunday and lived with family friends in Severodonetsk. On Monday, she and Anton met with Elisey and talked about the wedding and decided that it could take place on Friday. Since no wedding clothes could be found in this area so close to the war zone, Ruslana and Anton decided to buy matching T-shirts and jeans as their wedding attire. A ladies group from the Baptist church in Pervomaisk, which had regrouped in Severodonetsk, prepared the details of the wedding event, decorated simply, and baked and cooked for the celebration. And then on Friday, September 12, 2014, they had the wedding – and Ruslana became Anton's wife. Ruslana's parents could not come to the wedding, but they have embraced Anton as their son-in-law.

Shortly after the wedding, Anton received an invitation to take some Ukrainian children from the war zone to the United States of America. Anton received his visa and was able to take the group of children to the US in the spring of 2015. Ruslana, in the meantime, was trying to recover from the trauma she had experienced. They lived in Chernivtsi at this time, where Ruslana knew no one. It was a very dark time for her; she became depressed, felt physically exhausted from the ordeal of the previous months, and missed Anton terribly. Anton, meanwhile, attended church in the US and met a nice family, with whom he became good friends. When Anton came back to Ukraine, he stayed in touch with this family and their relationship deepened. Ministry in Ukraine continued during the spring and summer of 2015.

The US church also took a great interest in supporting Anton in his ministry in Ukraine. Anton did not know where to live, where to work, what to do. His calling was to minister to people. But going home to Pervomaisk was not an option; the city was occupied, the church had been burned down. Anton stayed in close contact with Elisey Pronin.

Elisey had already decided by this time to move his family to L'viv and to work at the seminary, UBTS. The Pronin had spent some time in the US recuperating from the war trauma they had experienced and moved to L'viv in the summer of 2015. Then Elisey invited Anton to join him in L'viv, do ministry together, and plant a new church. Ruslana and Anton decided to pray about this opportunity. They agreed that God's plan for them was to move to L'viv and join Elisey in his ministry. They moved to L'viv in the fall of 2015. Anton was able to share this ministry opportunity with the US church and with his American friends. The church decided to support Ruslana and Anton financially and also in prayer.

Ruslana and Anton are officially missionaries to L'viv. They are a huge asset at the church plant called *Disciples Church*. Anton is a deacon, Ruslana directs the children's ministry, and they host a small group in their home. They are also intensely involved in the youth ministry of the church, as well as bearing great responsibilities for the remodeling of the building that the church was just able to purchase. The traumatic war experience was emotionally challenging to work through, and Ruslana had many signs of post-traumatic stress. But now she and Anton enjoy a new life in L'viv and look to the future with joy and anticipation.

Ruslana reflected that her greatest spiritual growth took place as a result of the war in her home country and region. She said that due to the war and all that happened, she had to learn to depend on God more and more, because she realized that God was all she had in this traumatic time of escape and refugee life. Ruslana understands now that she really grew up spiritually during this time, walking by faith more than ever before.

CHAPTER EIGHT

Vika

Vika was born in the Donetsk region, but she grew up in Marinka, a small town in the Lugansk region. Her parents were her greatest influence, because they modeled a godly life to her and her siblings; they actively lived out their Christian faith. The family resided in their own house. They had bought the land and then started building a two-story home. It was a long process, over many years, because her father worked on the house while also working full-time as a gravestone mason, and part-time as a pastor.

During the summer, Vika would spend time outside, walking the streets, meeting friends, and greeting neighbors. She would play simple games on the streets, because they had no toys. They would play 'House' and 'Store', selling things to other kids. Every summer Vika would attend a Christian camp. She made new friends there; it was a time to hang out together, play games, and enjoy nature. Often the family would also go on a summer vacation to the sea. They would sometimes go to the Black Sea for recreation or to another seashore. Sometimes the family would even go to Crimea and spend seven to ten days at the beach.

As a young child Vika really wanted to go to school. She couldn't wait to start elementary school, and was excited when this season of her life finally began. In school, Vika liked mathematics a lot, especially algebra. Her preference for math had a lot to do with the teacher who Vika liked and who made the subject interesting. In school, she also had the opportunity to take music lessons and she sang in an ensemble. She really liked this singing group.

Having graduated from high school, she entered college and studied financial administration. Vika laughed and said this was not exactly her dream profession, but she chose this field, because she was good at math and with numbers. She studied at college for three years and received a diploma. Her college was in the Lugansk Region in a city called Kharkiv. After a fourth year, Vika received her master's degree.

Vika's father was the pastor in Marinka, a town about ten minutes away from Pervomaisk by car. Her church was small; only about fifty people attended. Vika went to church regularly; she did not have much of a choice, she giggled, as her dad was the pastor. She participated in Sunday school; eventually she helped with the Sunday school program.

The Baptist church in Pervomaisk was larger, with about 300 people in attendance; they also had more teenagers. This was attractive. Teenager Vika and her small youth group would always go to Pervomaisk Baptist Church for youth events; they did not have their own youth ministry in their hometown church. She joined the worship and praise group and enjoyed singing in this band. Vika really liked the youth club JAM (Jesus and Me) and enjoyed the opportunity to fellowship with other teenagers. Eventually, as she became an older teenager, she helped with the JAM club and with summer camp projects, as well.

Vika says that she grew up in a Christian family. Her father received Christ when she was just a baby. The family moved immediately as her father felt called to be a missionary to the Luhansk region. Vika herself became a believer during a Christian summer camp when she was eight years old. It was the last evening of the summer camp, Vika recalled; there was a big camp fire, lots of singing, and God touched her heart. She had to wait for her baptism until she was sixteen years old; this is a tradition in the Baptist churches in Ukraine. At her baptism she made a clear commitment to follow God and to serve in the church. She started a music ensemble with five people. She began to serve in her churches in Marinka and in Pervomaisk.

Vika had already left the area of Pervomaisk before the war started. Initially she studied at a university in Starobilsk, commuting every day; then she studied at a college in Kharkiv and lived in the dorm. She would spend the week studying at the university in Kharkiv, then return home every weekend. Eventually she got a job in the city and returned home less often, maybe once a month, to see family and friends. Often her sister Lena would come visit her in Kharkiv.

The last time she went home was in April 2014 during the Easter holidays in Ukraine. She was going to celebrate with her family and friends. Vika left after the holidays and went back to her studies in Kharkiv. She did not realize at the time that she was leaving her familiar life behind, never to return. In April 2014, all was still quiet and peaceful in her home town.

Her sister Lena came to visit her in Kharkiv again and stayed with Vika for a while; the sisters were planning to travel home together in July 2014. But their father, Igor, called them with bad news. He told them that it was not possible for them to come home. The unrest had started in their city, and her parents had moved into the basement and were living there. At this point, Vika said, she did not understand what was going on. Why could she not go home and see her family? Vika thought, "The last time I was home, everything was okay. What has happened?"

Lena and Vika stayed in Kharkiv and Lena started looking for work in the city. They kept calling their parents, getting updates from their hometown, watching the news on TV and the internet. At this point, Vika stated, the war did not touch her directly because she was living in Kharkiv. The sisters were just not able to travel home. She did not see shooting, but she followed the news, saw the blockades. She could not imagine that war had come to her small, insignificant village. She expected, like everyone else, that this unrest would last a short while, then peace and calm would be restored and everyone could go home. Everybody wanted to return to their quiet and peaceful village life again.

But the conflict escalated in the following weeks. Her father, known as a Baptist pastor, felt the threat of persecution from the new authorities. The whole family was in danger, so neither Vika nor her sister Lena could return to the city. Vika's father helped to evacuate people out of Pervomaisk and Marinka; he was a driver for those who wanted to escape from their town; all of them were becoming refugees in their own country. Her parents eventually joined the girls in Kharkiv, leaving their lives behind, choosing family and safety instead. They never returned to their hometown. All their belongings were left behind.

Vika's parents moved away from Kharkiv soon, as they had an invitation from Christian friends to live and work in Zaporizhzhia. They ended up living there for almost two years, until 2016. It was a great apartment for her parents, recalled Vika. They lived there rent-free, and only paid for water and gas. They were rebuilding their lives in this city. Her father worked as a part-time pastor and worked full-time in the gravestone business. Initially, only her father, mother, and brother Vova moved to Zaporizhzhia, but eventually Lena joined the family.

Vika said it was a very stressful time for her, because her parents pressured her to move to Zaporizhzhia. She wanted to be with her family, but she also really liked her university town, so Vika stayed in Kharkiv. She had a church home and friends in the city; she was working at her job and studying at the university. She paid for her own apartment and for her classes at the university. Vika was determined to finish her studies.

During these years, her parents prepared all the documents to emigrate to the United States. America had a program for the children of refugees. The goal was to get these kids to America and let them spend time at summer camps, relaxing and recuperating from the stress of experiencing war. Vika's parents prepared the necessary documents for their son Vova. Several children from Pervomaisk were offered this summer camp opportunity in the US. Vova, Vika's brother, received his visa and left for the US in the summer of 2015. He also received an invitation to study at an American high school. Vova stayed in America for three years of high school. He received his high school diploma and returned to Ukraine in the summer of 2018.

When Vika's parents were refused a visa to America, they accepted it as God's will. At this point, knowing that her parents were not moving to America, Vika decided to move to Zaporizhzhia. Life would be better to be together. Vika had enjoyed her independent life in Kharkiv. The move to Zaporizhzhia would be a big change for her. The city started a humanitarian aid center for refugees and Vika found work there. She started to build a life again in a new city, in a new ministry, with new work. She still thought that when things calmed down, they would all be returning to Marinka. But their hometown never became a quiet and peaceful place again.

Vika longingly said that she really wanted to get back for just a little while, to collect her documents, certificates, and diplomas. All of these things were left behind in their house. The family also had left behind all the photo albums. But a return was simply not possible. Their small town was in a war zone now, occupied by separatist forces. No one was safe, especially not a Baptist pastor's family. As far as she knows, she said, her house is still standing, and is not damaged by bombing. Other people live in her home now. Her grandma and grandpa are living in Donetsk, which is in the war zone, in the occupied territory.

Vika lived in Zaporizhzhia for one year. She worked and served in the local church and sang in a music group which performed at weddings and special events. Vika found a new rhythm to life and started to enjoy her new city. But then her parents decided to move the family to either Western Ukraine or Poland. When she found out about these plans, she felt anger and stress. Vika reasoned with her parents that she and Lena were already doing well here in Zaporizhzhia after the trauma of war; they had jobs and were rebuilding their lives. They had friends and enjoyed the fellowship at the church. They had just started putting down roots again. The sisters argued that maybe just their parents should move, and they would stay behind. This was an exciting prospect for the girls, allowing them to live by themselves and manage their own lives. But their father was convinced that God wanted the whole family to move together, possibly to L'viv.

Vika could not imagine uprooting her life again. There were many arguments, she recalled. Everybody agreed, though, to pray about the move. Vika said that L'viv was not her father's first choice. Igor took a trip to Poland to see if this would be a place for the family to live. He was invited to be a pastor in Poland and he visited this prospective church for several months. It was a small church that needed a lot of help. On his way back to Zaporizhzhia, Igor stopped in L'viv. Elisey Pronin, already living in L'viv by this time, suggested that Igor's family move to L'viv and help him with a new church plant.

Vika was not excited about moving to L'viv. In Zaporizhzhia, they had a rent-free apartment for two years. Life was good. Rental space in L'viv was limited and expensive. The family agreed that the move would hinge on one condition: if her father could find only a one-bedroom apartment for rent in L'viv, the girls would stay in Zaporizhzhia; but if God provided a bigger apartment for the family, they all would move to Western Ukraine. Vika and her family prayed about the apartment situation, especially during the time when Igor was looking in L'viv for a place to rent.

One morning, Igor called from L'viv and told the family what he had found – a three-bedroom apartment. It was a turning point for Vika, accompanied with many tears, because she clearly saw the development as God's answer to her prayers, even though it was not what she wanted to hear. The decision was made; the family was going to move together to L'viv. Vika acknowledged that "you can't ask God for guidance and provision, and then when He clearly gives it, reject it and choose your own way."

The family moved to L'viv in the summer of 2016. Vika still had university classes in Kharkiv to attend, so she was hoping to wait to move to L'viv after her classes finished. She pointed out to her father that train tickets from L'viv to Kharkiv were very expensive and a ticket from Zaporizhzhia to Kharkiv would be cheaper. She proposed moving to L'viv after her lectures finished in Kharkiv. But her father did not agree to this plan. He told her that she was moving now to L'viv. They would give her the money for the more expensive train trip to Kharkiv. Vika and her father went back and forth about this issue several times. Reluctantly, Vika agreed. This plan did not make sense to her, because it was clearly the more expensive option. But it was God's plan.

Her father picked her up from the train station the morning she arrived in L'viv and took her to the new apartment. Vika was not happy and she did not like the new apartment. Then they strolled around L'viv, to get to know the new city. That evening, Vika received a phone call from Olya Kiyan. Olya was working at UBTS already and told her that they needed workers at the seminary. She suggested that Vika should come for an interview the next day. Vika remorsefully recalled that just this morning she had arrived in L'viv and told God, "I don't like it here." By the evening of the same day, she had an invitation for a job interview. All she could say then was, "Thank you, God. Your plans are amazing. Your timing is perfect."

Vika said she had worried about finding work in L'viv, and had expected it to be very difficult as she was a refugee from the East and spoke Russian, not Ukrainian. Getting the job as an accountant at UBTS was really a miracle, she said. God worked in amazing ways, putting her new life together like a puzzle, with all the pieces falling into place. Vika is very happy that she is working in a Christian environment. UBTS is a thriving, exciting seminary. Her work is very challenging and intellectually stimulating. She really likes living in L'viv now; she feels greatly blessed by God.

Vika is also excited about the new church plant, Disciples Church, with Pastor Elisey Pronin. She is part of the worship team and helps with outreach, summer camps, and youth ministry. The new church has a lot of energy, Vika remarked, and people are open to doing things in new ways, trying new ministries, such as offering a coffee house, showing films, and reaching people through fun events. Vika fully embraces her new life in L'viv now. She lives with her siblings in a two-bedroom apartment. She is happy and thankful.

CHAPTER NINE

Lena

Lena was born in 1995 and grew up in Marinka, a small town not far from Pervomaisk. Everyone in the village basically knew each other; her family was known as the Baptist family. Lena said that her parents, Igor and Oksana, were good examples to her of serving God. She enjoyed a carefree childhood. Lena was very close to her older sister Vika, who modeled Christian faith and life for her. With their brother Vova, they formed a strong bond, like the three famous musketeers. Lena remembered their being a close family during her childhood.

Lena's parents worked, and her father was the bi-vocational pastor of the small village church. Her grandparents lived farther away, and several times during the year the children would go to the grandparents' house for vacation. Lena had many pets as a child, as the family lived in their own home and had a large yard. She recalled having dogs, cats, and even a guinea pig. They lived near a large forest, and the siblings would play there. With all their pets, it was never boring, said Lena, and they always found enough food to feed the pets.

Lots of kids lived on her street in Marinka; some of them were her friends at school. Lena would play with her friends in the streets, wander around town; they would explore together, play games and use their imagination; in the absence of toys they created a grocery store and "sold" food. Lena has fond memories of her childhood. Lena and her friends also invented a little business by creating small bouquets from the field flowers to sell for pennies on the side of the street to neighbors walking by. She said you felt like a millionaire when you sold one of those bouquets. Lena reminisced that as a child you have all the time in the world – you have no worries, and on the streets of her small village, life was lived without danger or fear. When it was time for dinner, her mom would simply call down the street, "Time to eat!" and Lena would rush home to a delicious meal with her family. She said this was the most happiest, carefree time in her life.

Elementary school was not to her liking, Lena admitted. Her time to play and roam freely was dramatically cut when school was in session. She was good at math and reading as a child, she remembered. She participated in a spelling and reading bee. Her memories of middle school were stronger. Lena had one good girlfriend, and they would do everything together - go to school together, walk home together, play together. It was a great friendship, because they got along so well and their personalities complemented each other. Math became more difficult for her in middle school. Many of her friends went to music lessons in Pervomaisk at the Baptist church.

Her dad's church was very small, mostly attended by dear old grandmas. This perpetuated a deep spiritual battle that was going on in her heart, Lena said. On the one side, she saw her parents going to church every Sunday, and expecting the children to attend with them of course; dad was, after all, the bi-vocational pastor of the small assembly. On the other side, Lena really did not want to attend church; she found it boring. She thought church was not really for her, only for old people, since young people did not attend her church, and there was no youth ministry. She talked with Vika about the situation and discovered that her sister felt the same way.

Lena's problem wasn't just that church was boring, it was that she didn't really see herself as a sinner, so she felt no need to repent. As a family, they would read the Bible every evening together, pray, and talk about the need for people to repent of their sins. Lena was thinking, "Yes, this is what bad people need to do, repent." Lena considered herself a Christian since she was growing up in a Christian family.

Her first convictions of personal sin came at the summer youth camps. Many of her friends who took music lessons at the church were going to these summer camps, so when Lena and her sister were invited to attend the camps, they went. At camp, students were given the opportunity to invite God into their lives. Lena observed with interest as many others made decisions for God, repenting of their sins, but she still considered herself a good person; she was even going to church every Sunday. But Lena recalled that she conducted her life as a hypocrite. On Sunday, she would be the holy Lena, going to church, being outwardly compliant and obedient to parents and God. At school, she was known as the daughter of the pastor in town. But Monday through Saturday, she would live like she wanted to live, drinking with classmates, and acting like an unbeliever.

When she was fourteen years old, an interesting thing happened. One of her friends in class confronted her about her double lifestyle. "How can you behave in such a way, but claim that you are a believer, a Christian? You behave worse than I do, and I certainly don't claim to believe in God." Lena said this confrontation was like a bucket of cold water poured over her. She realized that she was behaving like a hypocrite. When she wanted to act holy, she would tell people, "I go to church and my father is the pastor," but she couldn't care less about living the Christian truths and values. Lena said that during the summer months, acting like a Christian was easy because you were surrounded by all the believers in the summer camps and you would feel closer to God. But during the school year, you had to defend your faith, which made one not so popular.

Deep inside, the question tormented her: "Who are you really?" Lena was home one day and simply prayed and asked God to change her, to stop this double life she was beginning to hate. Lena said that from childhood on, she was afraid of hell. She did not love God, but the fear of being condemned to hell scared her. In Sunday school this idea of being punished and thrown into hell was a constant theme. Lena's dad would talk to her about heaven and hell. Her honest answer to herself would always be, "I don't really love God; I just don't want to go to hell."

But now, at the age of fifteen, Lena finally understood that she was not able to live a righteous life, that she did not have the strength to live without sinning. She asked God from a sincere heart to change her forever and to forgive her for her own sins. This repentance was accompanied with many tears, sorrow over her sin, and then rejoicing over her new life in Christ. From then on, she read her Bible every morning; before, she would just answer her dad, "Yes, yes, I read it this morning," lying to him without hesitation.

In the summer of 2010, Lena was baptized. After her baptism, she served in her dad's small church, started a group for girls, and created a worship team with her sister. Lena and Vika became acquainted with the young people in Pervomaisk, started participating and serving there, and enjoyed wonderful times of fellowship and camaraderie.

Her father was glad that Lena attended the church in Pervomaisk so frequently, and that she was involved in the youth ministry there. He had initially worried that Lena was hanging out with the wrong crowd of people and would be influenced away from God. The girls were drawn closer to God as they got to know people at the church. These personal connections and relationships made all the difference in Lena's life and her interest in the things of God. She started to participate in the youth group called JAM [Jesus and Me]. During the summer months, she was a helper at the children and teen camps. From then on, her life was consistent: at school she would tell others about her decision, she invited her friends to JAM, and she was the same person in public and in private, at school and at church. And church was no longer a boring place for old people.

After she finished high school, Lena really did not know where to go or what to study. Many parents, back then, would decide for their children what professional path they should take and where they should study. But Lena's parents told her, "This is your life; you choose what you want to do with it." But she wasn't sure, at the age of sixteen, what to do with her life.

Since many of her friends were heading to college, she decided to do the same. She started college in the fall of 2011. She wanted to study pedagogy, as this field seemed really interesting. The college, Lugansk National University, was located in the city of Starobilsk, more than two hours from Marinka by bus. But when Lena took the entrance exams, she was not accepted into the pedagogy program. Instead, she was invited to attend the music college and was offered a scholarship.

The decision was easy in the end, Lena remarked, because studying in the pedagogical department would cost the family too much money, while studies in the music college were free for her. The administration suggested that she could start her first semester in the music department of the university, and then they would switch her to the pedagogical department under the same conditions as in her musical studies - a full scholarship. This plan sounded really good to Lena. After a semester, though, she had such close friendships with her fellow students that she did not want to switch departments, so she stayed in the music program of the university. Lena enjoyed her classes; she played piano, learned how to direct an orchestra, and sang in the choir.

Lena studied for three years at the music college, from 2011 to 2014. She did not have to work during her college days; she was able to concentrate on her studies completely. She did not live in a dormitory during these years, either, but lived at home and commuted to school. Every day, she took several buses, the first one leaving at 5am, to travel from her small town to the city of Starobilsk, where the college was located; then she traveled the same way back at night. This was very tiring, Lena admitted. When she arrived home in the evening, all she wanted to do was sleep, but, of course, she had to do homework. This arrangement was favored by her parents, who really did not want her to live in the university dorms. For several years, Lena and Vika would do this trek to school together, as Vika was also studying in Starobilsk.

During Lena's third year at the music college, Vika moved to Kharkiv to continue her studies in that city. This was a difficult year for Lena, because Vika didn't come home too often anymore. Lena was able to visit her sister in Kharkiv for a week of vacation; it was a special time, but it was not like before, when they enjoyed such closeness, living together, traveling together to university every day, and sharing life.

In addition to Vika's moving to Kharkiv, Lena's brother Vova also moved away to his new school in Lugansk that specialized in sport education. Lena expressed great grief over this situation, as one moment the family was all together, and then, suddenly, she was the only one home. Vova thrived at the sports high school and won several trophies. After finishing this school, he was invited to attend a school in Kharkiv that trained future athletes.

Lena had finished her third year of studies at the university by the summer of 2014. Leading up to this summer, there were signs of increased conflict all around them. Every day Lena would travel through the street blockades, where she would see security forces, army equipment, and weapons. Four or five times on the way to the college, they would be stopped and asked to present their passports and other travel documents. Lena said she did not pay too much attention to the situation. She thought it was the Ukrainian army controlling the roads.

Then, during the summer months the situation got worse. The roadblock controls were everywhere now, and the conflict moved ever closer to their home town. Lena, already on summer break, wanted to visit Vika in Kharkiv for a week of vacation since Vika had not been able to get home in over two months. Vika still had to finish her exams, but afterwards, the sisters could travel home together and enjoy the summer in their village, living with Mom and Dad. Lena packed a small bag with summer clothes and headed by bus to Kharkiv, while her parents and her brother stayed home.

She arrived at Vika's dorm and settled in for the week. The next week, the parents called Lena and Vika and told them not to travel home, because the situation was getting too dangerous and unpredictable. The parents wanted their daughters to stay safely tucked away in Kharkiv for the time being. The week passed and the parents called again, advising the girls not to come home. The sisters were running out of money; the situation became really difficult, Lena said. No one really knew what to do or what would happen next. Everyone was still expecting that the conflict would blow over, and everyone would be able to return home for the summer.

Lena made an emphatic point to her parents, telling them that they should be leaving the village, for if it was not safe for her and Vika, it was certainly not safe for them, either. Their parents' decision to remain for now in the village, facing the danger, unsettled the girls and they were not able to sleep well at all, consumed with fear and worry for their loved ones.

Lena found a temporary job in Kharkiv, because she really needed some money. Vika had worked part-time during her studies and had some small income from this job. The sisters were still thinking that soon they would be returning home. Lena was concerned how to finish her university studies; she had only so far completed the third year of her education. To receive a bachelor's degree, she needed one more year in the music college.

Two months passed this way, the parents reiterating again and again for the sisters to stay in Kharkiv and not return home. It was a very strange situation for Lena, living for two months without her parents, managing life by herself, earning money to live. The living conditions also became more difficult; Vika had a very small room in the dorm, and another friend from Pervomaisk arrived and needed shelter. Two other students slept in the dorm room as well; the facility was overrun with refugees. Mattresses were spread out on the floor, and people lived like sardines, stacked on top of each other.

Lena's parents called, informing the girls that they were finally leaving their home town. They would be moving to Zaporizhzhia. Lena did not understand why her parents were resettling there. She thought, "I have a job; I will just stay with Vika." Lena's mom called at the beginning of September 2014, ordering Lena to get on the bus the next day and move to Zaporizhzhia. Lena was not happy about this directive from her parents. She wanted to stay in Kharkiv, be with her sister. What was there in Zaporizhzhia for her?

Vika was allowed to stay in Kharkiv to continue her studies and work her part-time job - for the time being. Lena reluctantly moved to Zaporizhzhia. Vova, her brother, had moved with his parents, too; but through an exchange program with American churches and organizations, Vova was able to go to the USA for two months as a refugee child affected by the conflict. This group of Ukrainian children was chaperoned by Anton, Ruslana's husband-to-be.

In Zaporizhzhia, Lena began a temporary new life. Her parents found work making gravestones. She wondered how to continue her studies. Would it be possible to do the courses online? It turned out not to be a viable option, because the students could not return to the university to take their exams. Lena did not return to her studies that fall but looked for work to supplement the family income.

The cost of living was higher in Zaporizhzhia, and the family had many expenses, paying rent, buying food, needing clothes for the winter. Through some good friends, her mom found out that there was a job opening in the humanitarian aid center for refugees. The director initially invited Lena to help at the center as a volunteer, but the work eventually turned into a full-time job with pay for her. The pay was much smaller than Lena would have earned at a regular job, but she decided to stay and put all her efforts into the on-going humanitarian crisis.

Lena lived in Zaporizhzhia for two years, working at the humanitarian center. She and her family were some of the first refugees to arrive in the region; many others followed over the next few years. The city was often the first stop for many refugees. At the center, many people needed practical help, such as medical assistance, food, finances, and clothing. They sought advice from the counselors and tried to find a new direction for their lives. Lena would daily work from 9 a.m. to 2 p.m., and roughly 700 people would go through the center daily. The center did many projects, as well, undergirded by the American organization Caritas. Lena eventually started working by contract directly for Caritas, and her income increased.

Lena remembered that the refugees had many baffling questions: What was going on? When could they return home? Where would they live temporarily? Where should they go next?

Many were greatly distressed emotionally. The center provided great quantities of food, clothing, shoes; its staff also shared the gospel with the desperate people and organized Bible studies for them.

Lena was part of a volunteer group from the center, which took supplies to the war zone in the Lugansk region. On one of these trips, she was about five miles from her home, and she could see her town in the distance; this is the closest she ever came to being home again. Her family has never returned to their town or the neighboring city of Pervomaisk, she said with a sigh.

A core group of refugees met for daily worship. A small Baptist church existed in Zaporizhzhia already, and Lena started serving in the church. She sang in the choir, helped with the youth group, got to know the other young people, and enjoyed the fellowship. Lena said for young people these traumatic times were a little easier to handle than for the older generation. In many cases, parents and grandparents had built their homes themselves, had invested all their energy - and often, all their money - into their houses; their lives were tied up in the East.

The younger generation made the best out of the crisis. Lena began to enjoy Zaporizhzhia. She made new friends, became part of a church and a youth group again, and was actually glad to live in a bigger city with more choices and opportunities than her small town of Marinka offered. This new place was becoming home. After Lena had lived in Zaporizhzhia for one year, her sister Vika finally moved there, as well, having finished her bachelor's degree in Kharkiv. Lena's brother Vova was still in America, now studying at an American high school. Vika still needed to travel occasionally to Kharkiv for master's degree classes, but Lena was happy at this point, having her dear sister living with them again. Another year passed - Lena spent all of 2015 in Zaporizhzhia.

Then Lena's dad contemplated moving the family to Poland. Igor lived in Poland for two months, feeling out the situation, seeing if he could find work. He wanted a stable life for his family. The "Polish option" did not pan out. Lena's dad left Poland and stopped in L'viv on his return trip, having received an invitation from Elisey Pronin to see him. Elisey had, by this time, returned from the US and had moved his family to L'viv in the summer of 2015. He worked at UBTS. Igor and Elisey knew each other well, having been pastors in neighboring towns in the East. Elisey invited Igor to move to L'viv and work with him in the start of a new church.

When Lena's dad returned home, he told the family that they would be moving to L'viv. Lena's response was less than enthusiastic. She did not want to leave the familiar and comfortable life that they had built over the last two years. Lena said she had everything she could wish for: many friends, a nice apartment, a good church, a worship team, a good job. The thought of leaving all she had in Zaporizhzhia, to move to L'viv where she had no friends, no church, and no work, was unthinkable. For the longest time, she and Vika would cry and beg their dad not to move the family to L'viv. To leave Zaporizhzhia was the most difficult decision to make, said Lena, considering all they would lose – again.

Igor did not really want to move without his girls; leaving them behind was not an option for him. He told his daughters, that they did not have to move, but that it was the will of God for their family to go to L'viv, and they should really follow God's leading. Lena said she had a choice and, at the same time, did not have a choice.

Lena's dad left to find an apartment for the family in L'viv. He told Lena and Vika that they needed to let him know soon about their decision; it would influence the size of the apartment he would try to rent. Friends had told them it was generally difficult to find an apartment in L'viv; it could take months of searching. However, Lena's dad found a big apartment for the family within a week of his arrival in L'viv; the rent per month was surprisingly low. Igor called home and told the family the news. This call caused many tears, because now Lena and Vika knew that they had to move to L'viv. They were very upset for a long time. But Lena and her sister did understand and accept that this path was God's way of leading the family; L'viv would be okay.

Lena well remembered that her thoughts were reasonable, but her emotions were in rebellion against these plans. She was not willing to leave friends, jobs, church, and youth group. Lena did not want to start a new life somewhere again, having had this experience of resettling already in Kharkiv and in Zaporizhzhia. She prayed to God for a way out, a way for her to stay in Zaporizhzhia. Her current employer even offered her higher wages and said he would pay for her rent, so she could stay.

But Lena and Vika moved and joined their parents in L'viv in September 2016. Lena remembered arriving at the main train station and meeting her parents. For a whole week, all Lena could do was cry. She was so unhappy about the move to L'viv. The weather was terrible, foggy, rainy and nasty. She felt very unwelcome in L'viv. When she saw the apartment for the first time, she shuddered, as it was full of old furniture. She sighed, "O God, why am I here?" The first three months in L'viv were very difficult for Lena. She could not see any future for her in this city. She felt depressed and questioned God's wisdom and her parents' decision. She could not find work and would sit at home for hours, just staring out the window, crying. Emotionally and physically, she was depleted, lacking energy for even the smallest chores.

It continued to rain a lot in L'viv that fall, which deepened her depressive mood even further. She was trying to figure out what had happened with her life and what she was supposed to do with it now. Lena said she asked herself: What should I do? Where should I work? Why even study? For what purpose? She was experiencing real depression. She was still trying to cope with all the trauma and loss over the last few years by looking at some old photographs and old letters, remembering the better times of a previous life. Lena was unwilling to start over again in L'viv; she lingered in the past with the memories of her old life.

Lena went with her family to the Baptist seminary, UBTS, where a small group of believers was meeting for Bible study under Elisey's leadership. This small assembly could become a church plant with a Sunday worship service, Elisey imagined. Elisey also told Lena and her family that he would like to see a youth group or youth ministry being started out of the Bible study. Initially the group was called Project Disciples. The plans for renting space, forming teams, starting a praise and worship band were discussed at this time. Pretty soon, Lena and Vika began to serve in the church plant, singing for worship, engaging young people. Serving actually helped Lena get out of her depression, because her focus moved outward, toward meeting others' needs, rather than constantly focusing inward, concentrating on her own suffering.

Another good decision she made during the last quarter of 2016 was to enroll as a student at UBTS in the international missions program. Lena said that she had thought about missions since her childhood and was fascinated by the wide world; she always wanted to be a missionary. Lena liked the first few sessions she had at UBTS. She met some new people in her courses and made new friends.

During a November class, Lena came to a turning point in her struggle with L'viv. She was finally able to say, "Thank you, God, for bringing me to L'viv." This moment changed Lena's whole outlook on the situation - and her new life in Western Ukraine. She fully accepted that this life in L'viv was God's will for her, that God had plans for her and beyond her, here and now. God was showing her that He would use her talents and gifts to serve Him in L'viv. Lena could stop thinking only about the past and anticipate her future with God in this new place.

Lena's life soon got busier. The church plant, *Disciples Church,* started officially with worship services Sunday afternoons in the library of UBTS. Since the library was only available Sunday afternoons, all other events for the small church plant would be held at Disciples Territory, an off-site space the church rented. Lena worked there as a room manager. She stayed busy with church-related work all the time. *Disciples Church* gave her a small salary for her work, which helped her family with the cost of living in L'viv. She worked in the office, met with young people, organized events, such as discussion groups and game nights. She studied at UBTS, doing her homework faithfully.

Lena reflected about this time in her life and said that life became good, fairly comfortable, and stable again; she had a good routine. She said she began to like her life in L'viv. By the time she celebrated her first Christmas and New Year's Eve in L'viv, she was very glad, almost happy, with her life, seeing it as a blessing from God. Lena was actually surprised about all the possibilities and opportunities that God had opened up for her and her team to work and serve in the church. She began to understand that her ministry could be greater and better than anything she had done before.

Thanks to her studies at UBTS, she enjoyed a lot of good, deep fellowship with solid, strong Christians. Through interesting lectures and new close friendships Lena grew spiritually and recovered emotionally. God showed her more of His plans for her life, and a subtle excitement filled Lena with hope for the future. She took time to reflect upon the experiences she had lived through. She got to know herself better through introspection and through good discussions with friends. Most of her family was together in one place. Vika had found work as an assistant accountant at the seminary, her mom and dad worked at their jobs; only Vova was away, still studying at an American high school.

All the mission students of UBTS were told that by the second year they would go somewhere for a missions practicum. Initially, Lena thought that she would not be able to go; she had no job at the moment that would finance such a practicum. One of her classmates told her to pray about a place of service and the needed financial support for such a project and trust God with the rest. This was a good reminder for Lena to pray about every aspect of her life and trust God. She began to pray in earnest every day about her missions practicum.

One of Lena's classmates, Julia, mentioned that she was thinking about a missions practicum, as well, and needed to team up with someone. Over dinner, Lena and Julia sat down to talk more about their ideas. Julia wanted to go to the Middle East, while Lena was really interested in serving in Africa. Lena was wondering how God could bring their very diverse interests together. When Lena mentioned that she also really liked the country of Georgia, Julia's enthusiastic response was, "Oh, me too!" This was the starting point for Lena and Julia to talk, pray, and prepare for Georgia. They researched the spiritual needs in Georgia and presented the country in their missions class. After a month of prayer, Julia and Lena were invited to be mission volunteers in Georgia for four months.

One complicating factor for Lena was her intense involvement at *Disciples Church*. In May of 2017, she sat down with her pastor Elisey, and as they filled out some UBTS paperwork, she mentioned that she was planning to go on a longer mission trip, really a mission practicum, to the country of Georgia, and asked if he would give his blessing to these plans. They agreed that the practicum should take place in the fall of that year. The young church plant had already made many plans for summer camps, in which Lena was deeply involved, so her practicum wouldn't start till after the summer months were over. This was a win-win situation for all. It gave Lena time to serve the church plant and raise money for her practicum.

Lena went to Georgia, initially planning to serve four months, but she ended up staying there for seven months. She arrived in Georgia with Julia at the end of August 2017. Lena prayed that she would not just be teaching others, but would be learning from the people as well. She wanted to be kind and friendly to people, to share freely about her life with God, and to serve in whatever capacity opened up. Lena ended up working in partnership with a local church; she also connected to the ministry of InterVarsity, reaching university students with the gospel. Lena served in children's clubs, assisted groups of disabled people, and hiked and explored nature with teens and young adults. Lena saw God using her to be part of His work in Georgia.

Lena pointed out that God does not need super-spiritual people; He uses those who are willing to follow and obey Him and surprises them with a life they could not have imagined apart from Him.

Her time in Georgia taught her to trust God more fully than ever before. Sometimes finances were very tight. She built relationships with people. She tried to listen to what God – only God – was saying to her; she chose not to listen to well-meaning people with bad advice. She spent much time in prayer, fasting, seeking God, alone with her Bible. There were so many opportunities to serve and be engaged in people's lives. But the culture and customs of Georgia were very different than what she was used to in Ukraine. The mission volunteers had come to the country to work with orthodox people, but God brought so many Muslims into their lives. Seeing a Muslim girl daily reading the Bible is a memory Lena will treasure forever. "Wow," Lena's thought, "What God can do!"

Lena did not want to return to Ukraine at all. She loved her work and ministry in Georgia and saw God at work in the people around her. Lena compared the stress of this time leading up to her eminent return to Ukraine with the stress of leaving Zaporizhzhia. She had found a new life in Georgia; was God really asking her to give it up again? The time came to return to Ukraine. Tickets were bought, things were packed up, the suitcases were ready. Lena said she thought then that she would just go home to Ukraine for a little while and return to Georgia as soon as possible. But she admitted not having conferred with God about these plans. She wondered why God would remove her from such a fruitful ministry setting. Her departure from Georgia was very emotional and teary.

In March of 2018, Lena returned to L'viv. She wanted to work with university students, so she started a weekly discussion group for students. She also led other events at the Disciples Territory meeting room. She found part-time summer work as the administrator of a children's center. In the fall, after the university holidays, she reopened the discussion club for students with a small team of young people from *Disciples Church*. Lena met one young Ukrainian woman who had lived in Georgia for five years with her family as missionaries. This woman was working with InterVarsity, on college campuses, engaging students in discussion groups. She prompted Lena to think about working with InterVarsity in Ukraine. Lena's first reaction was, "What? No, not me." But this lady challenged her not to just write the idea off, but to pray about it. Lena prayed and thought about the opportunity with InterVarsity all that week. She talked with her pastor Elisey about the ministry of InterVarsity. God had directed her life so far, Lena said. Now He was stirring a desire in her heart to serve Him full-time as a missionary with InterVarsity.

Lena was invited to attend an InterVarsity conference in Kyiv, and shortly thereafter, she decided to begin ministry with InterVarsity to college campuses in L'viv, Ukraine. The team of InterVarsity missionaries has regular training and education conferences to equip their staff for their ministries. Lena greatly enjoys her work with InterVarsity in Ukraine, and her fellow missionaries have become dear friends to her. Her financial support is not fully raised yet. *Disciples Church* supports her work at InterVarsity monthly.

Lena is still studying at UBTS. She cannot say right now where her future lies – in student ministry or in international missions. But one thing she affirmed strongly: she wants to follow God, no matter where He leads her. She is convinced that you can be happy in the place where God has planted you. Ministry is possible wherever you are, and God will use you as He pleases.

Looking back, Lena said, she sees that God was faithfully leading her. Her life experience has given her the confidence to trust God for her future, no matter where and how. God has worked all things for good. At present, Lena lives with her sister Vika and her brother Vova in a small apartment and they enjoy close fellowship with each other and do ministry together at *Disciples Church*.

CHAPTER TEN

Veronika

Veronika grew up in Pervomaisk, in the Lugansk region. She was the second born of four siblings. Her father worked as a driver; her mom worked part-time as a nurse. The family lived first in a small house, but in 1998, when she was eight years old and had already started school, her parents bought a bigger house that needed a lot of repairs. Veronika remembered that the repairs to the house took so long, that by the time it was finished in 2012, she already had left home and was married.

Veronika's parents were strong believers; as far back as she can remember, they went to church. Every Sunday, she attended worship services, her father served as a deacon in the church, her mom led the choir. Her father has an excellent baritone voice and often sang solos. Her father even managed a little ensemble. Her parents were modeling to her how to be servants in the church. Due to her parents' example, Veronika wanted to serve in the church, too. She went to Sunday school and Christian summer camps.

One Christmas season, the church prepared a Christmas play, and she was chosen to play Mary. Veronika went to pastor Elisey and asked him to explain the role of Mary; she wondered how she could play the role of Mary even though she had not repented of her sin. Elisey helped her understand her need for salvation, and she repented and received Jesus as Lord and Savior; she was ten years old. According to her church's policy, she couldn't be baptized at this age; she needed to wait till she was almost 16. Veronika was baptized in 2005.

Veronika finished school in 2008 and began her studies at the foreign language institute, Horlivka Institute for Foreign Languages (Donbass State Pedagogical University). Veronika returned from her studies in

Horlivka every weekend to her hometown of Pervomaisk. She sang in the choir on Sundays as part of her ministry, even while away in college. She finished university in 2012 with a bachelor's degree in foreign languages.

Veronika met Artur in youth group at church when she was a young teenager. While Veronika grew up in church and in a Christian family, Artur, on the other hand, came to faith through a youth outreach program; he followed his profession of faith in Jesus by being baptized in Pervomaisk. Artur was five years older than Veronika. They spent time together in Sunday school and youth group. While Artur was studying at a Christian Institute in Kherson, they did not see each other much. But there was already a spark between them. Artur came back to the region in 2008 for his friends' wedding. At that time, Veronika was eighteen years old. From then on, Veronika and Artur stayed in touch by phone, and basically dated for three years this way. Eventually, they planned their wedding with her parents' blessing. They married in 2011. Veronika said they would have married earlier, but her parents did not approve of an earlier date.

There were challenges in their young married life; but the problems were nothing compared to the trials they would face in the near future. Their oldest son Benjamin was born in 2012. With his birth, life as a mom and homemaker began. They lived near the church in the small city of Pervomaisk. Elisey Pronin was the pastor of the Baptist church. When Benjamin was a month old, Veronika stepped back into church ministries again, having the help of her mother-in-law, who babysat Benjamin. Veronika sang in the choir, which her mother conducted and in which many of her siblings participated, as well. It was a family affair. Together with her older brother, she started a youth club called JAM, Jesus and Me. At the JAM club they would sing songs, play games, and study the Bible. Artur was helping with the Bible study part of JAM. The young people had an opportunity to fellowship, get to know each other, and even go on summer camps together for more fellowship and Bible teaching.

During the week, Artur went to work, and Veronika and Benjamin stayed busy at home, often visiting her parents who lived only 10 minutes away. Veronika remembered that in Pervomaisk you could do everything on foot because the city was so small, everybody was friendly, you always had help. Veronika recalled that she could simply call a Christian brother or sister from the church, and they would come over, put Benjamin in the stroller, and go for walk with him, so she could do some ministry in the church, enjoy a break, cook, or get some cleaning done. The family of God helped each other in practical ways; it was a way of life for all of them.

Veronika was a young mom when everything began to change for her in 2013; the unrest had started in Kyiv. Then the conflict spread to Slovyansk, still about fifty miles from Pervomaisk. Veronika remembered that no one thought that the political crisis would affect their lives, or that war would come to their city. Friends and acquaintances came to visit them in Pervomaisk, telling them about the situation in Slovyansk. Veronika saw no evidence of the military in her city at the beginning of 2014.

Russia annexed Crimea in March 2014; then Crimea underwent the so-called referendum and separated from Ukraine, becoming part of Russia. People in Pervomaisk suddenly started to talk about a referendum for the Lugansk region.

One of the first shocks Veronika remembered was when she received a call from Artur, who told her that the brothers and sisters were called to the church to protect the building. No one really knew what was going on, but everyone knew that the church had to be protected. It was the first phase of fear for Veronika; she knew that war was coming to her city. This war was coming into their lives, their home, their church. The church building was only a five-minute walk from their house. The church brothers organized themselves into groups to guard the church.

Veronika still did not see any military on the streets of Pervomaisk. She said they continued to live their daily lives, but with fear and worry. Her friends and family experienced check points and street blockades. Her sister was studying music and had to travel to a neighboring town every week. She had to show her passport every time she went back and forth between the blockades. Veronika herself did not see these blockades since she was home with Benjamin. Some news outlet said that the Ukrainian army would dissolve the blockades; this claim was repeated often, but nothing really happened.

Spring 2014 came to their small town and life continued, but it was a strange "new normal". When people tried to leave the city, they were stopped and their cars were confiscated. The travelers had stored all their belonging in the cars; now these vehicles were taken, along with everything in them. The citizens had no option but to return home with nothing.

The town itself was eerily quiet, Veronika remembered. Veronika's husband Artur had no work at this time, so he was home a lot. They had to be careful about spending their money. Artur suggested that they should leave; maybe they could go stay with friends and return when the crisis was over. Veronika and her family were some of the first folks to leave town. Only one other family had left already; their neighbors would leave a month later. Veronika really did not want to leave because Pervomaisk was home, but Artur persisted. Since they owned no car with which to leave, her dad drove the family to the train station. They took the train to a nearby city and lived with Artur's relatives for two weeks.

Veronika's brother and his bride had planned their wedding day long before the conflict broke out. Veronika and her family took the train to the Ivanov Frankivsk region to attend the celebration. But the ever-present question was what to do next. Was returning to Pervomaisk an option at this point? What was going on back home? Since they did not know if and when they could return to Pervomaisk, they chose to stay in Ivanov Frankivsk till further plans could be made, but with no job and no permanent place to live, this was not a long-term plan. Veronika's father returned home to Pervomaisk after the wedding.

Veronika and Artur called friends in Rivne and asked if they could come stay with them. The friends told them that they were actually not in Rivne right now, but in a summer camp. But their friends connected Veronika's family with another Christian family who gladly invited them for a short stay. Veronika, Artur, and little Benjamin took the train to Rivne, and stayed with that family for several days.

The family treated them very kindly and showed real interest in their lives. They asked them questions, provided for their needs, fed them, provided a place to sleep, and showed them sympathy for their situation. But their hosts also expected that Veronika and Artur would do as they were told in regard to their own faith practice, which meant head coverings, women wearing skirts, and attending the Pentecostal church. Artur really wanted to find work, but their hosts told him, "Why work? Just serve God." This was the moment when Artur decided that they could not stay with this family very long. They really needed a place of their own, and renting an apartment became a driving desire for Veronika and Artur.

For the next few weeks, the family would live with different members of the church, one week here, two weeks there. Often, one room was made available for Veronika, Artur, and little Benjamin, while their hosts slept in another room. Artur still had not found work. Finances were very tight. Finally, Artur found work, but even with some income, life was difficult. The cost of living around Rivne was much higher than in the East of Ukraine. Their Baptist friends ended up staying at the summer camp for one more month and allowed Veronika's family to move into their apartment and live there till their return. This family finally came back from summer camp and needed to use their own apartment again.

Artur needed to find an apartment for his small family, but try as he might, he couldn't secure an apartment. No one would rent rooms to refugees, expecting them to leave again soon. Finally, with help from the Baptist church, they found a one-bedroom apartment, though it was in a horrible building in a bad neighborhood. Veronika remembered that the flat was empty, no beds, no wardrobe, nothing. They had no belongings, no furniture, just a couple of suitcases for the road. The believers from the church collected things for them and brought them a bed, a wardrobe, a refrigerator, pots and pans for the kitchen, dishes and cutlery. The church family gave generously and met their very basic needs. The believers also brought produce and food staples that they needed. Veronika said they really had nothing to live on themselves. At this point, the family had been on the road for two months already. God had provided for their needs through the family of God in the churches.

Once, a sister in the Baptist church invited Veronika to her home while Artur was at work. Veronika had been home alone, taking care of Benjamin. She gladly accepted the invitation to get to know someone. They had time to drink coffee and enjoy some fellowship. Veronika walked home with Benjamin to their small apartment, but when she arrived she was shocked to find there had been a robbery.

Someone had given Veronika and Artur a laptop and a backpack in which they stored their money and documents. When she opened the door upon returning home from her outing, she saw that the laptop and backpack, along with all their savings, their official documents and passports, were gone. It was too much to take. Who would steal from refugees on the run?

In reflection, Veronika wondered if she was being watched. The thieves must have paid careful attention to notice when she was not home. Several times before, the doorbell would ring, but no one was there. She found cigarette butts repeatedly on the kitchen floor. Her best guess was that her neighbors gained access into their apartment several times. Only the neighbors down the hall could disappear into their apartment quickly after using the doorbell. Their landlord did not want to deal with the situation.

Life was hard, Veronika remembered. Finances were tight, especially after the robbery. Artur's brother came to visit from Moscow and brought them $200. The believers in the church took care of the family and met their needs. Different churches were ministering to them in various ways. One church had given Artur a job, the Baptist church provided their apartment furnishings, and other churches provided humanitarian aid. They lived four months in Rivne, then made plans to move to Poland. They were told that Arthur could find work in Poland during the summer months. They also had Ukrainian friends in Poland, who had emigrated. At this time, Veronika found out that she was expecting her second child. This was a big surprise. After thinking and praying, they decided to move to Poland in 2015.

Poland had opened some refugee camps. One option for Veronika and her family was to live in a summer camp made available for refugees from Ukraine. They didn't need a visa for Poland, Veronika remembered, because they had official refugee status. A family from the Rivne church drove them to the border and left them there with all their belongings. They had quite a few bags and luggage pieces by now. Artur told the border guards that they were refugees. The border proceedings were long and tiresome for the refugees. It took eight or nine hours, Veronika recalled. They were also moved around between two different border crossings. They had to answer many questions and had to explain where they were going. Finally, they were granted entrance into Poland.

The information they had previously received was that once in Poland, transportation to the summer camps would be provided for refugees. They had been instructed that when they passed through the border, they were to travel immediately to the summer camp. But by now, it was late afternoon. Veronika was already four months pregnant; it had been a long and draining day. Little Benjamin also had had enough. Because of the long delay in crossing the border, no transportation to the summer camps was available. Veronika, emotionally drained, felt abandoned. They couldn't go back to the Ukrainian side of the border, because their Ukrainian friends had left, returning to Rivne. On the Polish side, however, they had no way to get where they were going. She melted into a pool of tears.

The Polish border guards told them that there was a bus going to Lublin from the bus terminal. So, Veronika and her small family had to take a taxi from the border to the bus terminal, then scout out the right bus and find room for all their belongings on a bus meant to transport only passengers. They made it to Lublin at dusk. They hoped for the next connection, whether bus or train. They called some friends, asking for help to figure out transportation to the camp. When they learned that no more trains or buses were going to their destination that day, Veronika broke down in tears. She remembered that they stood on the street, surrounded by their luggage. Benjamin was crying; they were all exhausted. She was at the end of her rope.

But God's family came to the rescue again. Artur called one Christian sister who had immigrated from Pervomaisk to Warsaw. This lady called her friend in Lublin, and this friend called another friend; eventually a Polish Catholic family arrived at the Lublin bus terminal to collect Veronika and her family. They had to make two trips from the train station to the apartment to transport all the luggage because they had a small car. This hospitable family did not speak Ukrainian or Russian, and Veronika's family did not speak Polish. Their hosts bought them train tickets and took them to the train station the next morning. And finally, they arrived at the summer camp for refugees.

They lived at the camp for one month. As more and more refugees came, the conditions in the camp became worse and worse. This camp received not only Ukrainian refugees, but also refugees from other countries. Bad things were happening in these camps; it was not safe to live there. Veronika said it was especially challenging to live there with a small child. She desperately wanted to leave the camp. Through Polish friends they found out that near Gdansk a small room was available for rent. The only real cost would be for utilities, water and gas. This seemed a good possibility to Veronika. Artur could work and earn enough money for a living. The family bought tickets to travel to the south of Gdansk, to a small town called Malbork.

When they arrived, their host met them. He was a 70-year-old Christian brother. They understood each other poorly, because they did not speak Polish. The older gentleman spoke some Russian, and they were able to communicate a little bit. Their host first took them to his own house, not the area where the apartment was. This made them suspicious.

Veronika's family sat down in the living room and waited. What was going to happen next? Was there a room available for rent or not?

Their host asked them how much money they had to live on. After hearing their answer, he told them they would need to live with him, that they didn't have enough money. He was building a private room for his mother in the back of the property, but it was not finished. Veronika's family could live there. In the evening, his wife arrived; she did not know anything about these plans. When her husband told her that this family was going to live with them, it was a shock to her. Artur and Veronika moved in and stayed - for seven months.

They helped their hosts to finish the room, and Artur did much of the physical labor. Their second son Samuel was born in Poland in 2015. The host family helped the Ukrainian refugees in many ways. Veronika needed a doctor during the pregnancy, but she did not speak Polish. Their hosts, themselves retired doctors in the fields of dentistry and family medicine, had friends who specialized in gynecology. Artur worked and earned money. But ultimately the situation was unsustainable, as the two elderly people wanted peace and quiet, while Veronika's family consisted of two small children with lots of energy and loud voices.

The question arose again – where to live? Veronika's parents had returned to Pervomaisk after the wedding in Ivanov Frankivsk. Could they return, too? But her parents wrote to Veronika, telling her that after living underground for ten months, they were leaving Pervomaisk. Veronika's mom had blood pressure problems due to the stress of war and the constant experience of fear due to the occupation of their home town. Veronika's siblings were spread out across Ukraine. One brother was married in Ivanov Frankivsk, two of her siblings had stayed with him after the wedding. Veronika's youngest brother Sergey had been in Kyiv at a camp the entire time. Life was so stressful for him emotionally, that his hair turned gray at age fourteen.

Veronika and Artur had lived in Gdansk with the elderly couple for seven months. Another move became necessary. One Ukrainian believer, Maxim, was Artur's friend and helped Artur to find work and an apartment to rent near Gdansk. Veronika's parents also arrived in Poland. They had organized a choir and were on tour in Poland, telling the Ukrainian war story to Polish churches through songs. Veronika and her parents met in Gdansk, and the grandparents met little Samuel for the first time. Veronika's parents kept traveling, going to Germany and Switzerland, sharing the Ukrainian story. Her brother Mark lived with Veronika for a while. Artur was able to work a lot, and her little boys, Benjamin and Samuel, had an uncle to play with.

At the local Baptist church, Veronika enjoyed fellowship with other young women, while their kids played with each other. Veronika said it took her two bus rides to get to church with her little boys, but it was worth the effort for the sweet fellowship she experienced there and the emotional and psychological support she received among believers. Veronika was able to make real friendships with people who were in a similar situation to hers.

When their rent was raised, Veronika and Artur had to move yet again. They found a less expensive, and even better, apartment in Gdansk. Again, this apartment was empty, but with the help of local believers, the place was furnished simply. Even the landlord was friendly and supplied some furniture. Veronika worked for an hour or two, cleaning apartments in the building, while the children were sleeping. She didn't earn much money, but they got a reduction on their rent.

Veronika did not really like Gdansk. Artur spent long days at work while she was just home with the kids; when he would finally come home, she really needed some time by herself. She would go to the park and eat sweets. In Poland, kindergarten isn't free, so they could not afford for Samuel or Benjamin at attend. Veronika put a lot of effort into learning Polish. A Polish believer gave her free lessons, and she learned to speak Polish from simply being in the community and in the Polish Church.

After living in Gdansk for one year, they were faced with yet another decision about relocation. The family had started the paperwork to stay in Poland permanently. It was a complicated bureaucratic process. Veronika recalled that it was a very stressful time, because they did not know what was going to happen to their family next. They had to go to the post office regularly and check to see if they had mail from the government. A letter would eventually decide what was going to happen. They were hoping to receive a permanent visa for Poland. After much waiting, worrying, and hoping, their permanent visa was denied. By 2016, they had received another notification telling them it was time to leave Poland. They decided to return to Ukraine, choosing L'viv as their next destination, because by this time, Veronika's parents were living there. Veronika's pastor, Elisey Pronin from Pervomaisk, had relocated with his family to L'viv as well.

Veronika's family moved from Gdansk, Poland, to L'viv, Ukraine, in October of 2016. Initially, they lived with Veronika's parents in a house on the outskirts of L'viv. She recalled that they were grateful for this home, as they could not afford their own place. Veronika's youngest brother also lived with them in L'viv. Her parents submitted some documents to the housing administration, stating that their current home was too small for a family of seven, soon-to-be-eight, with the addition of Veronika's sister Lena. For one year, they lived together in two small rooms. Eventually, God blessed her parents with another apartment in the city. Her brother and sister moved with their parents to the new apartment. Veronika and Artur stayed with Benjamin and Samuel in the house and finally had a home to themselves.

Veronika long ago stopped counting how often she has moved. Life has been very difficult. But now, looking back, she sees God's hand, how He takes care of His own. During the most difficult circumstances, God sent them people who would help. God repeatedly used believers to bless them. Countless times they experienced His mercy and grace. "God was teaching me to trust Him, and I was learning to trust Him," reflected Veronika.

Before, in Pervomaisk, life was normal, simple, stable. They had problems, but nothing earth shattering. The last four years of her life had been anything but stable, she admitted. Even now, she wouldn't describe her life as normal, she said. Artur is constantly looking for work to provide for the family. Refugees receive a small amount of financial aid from the government to pay for an apartment. "God is continuing to teach us to trust Him," she said. Their third son, Luka, was born in August of 2018.

In L'viv, Veronika and her family are part of the church plant Disciples Church, and once again, Elisey Pronin is her pastor. Her parents are also in the church, as well as her younger brother and her sister. Veronika doesn't make long term plans, she admitted, because life changes so much and is so unpredictable. She does not really know how to plan anything anymore. She has dreams for the future, but she focuses on creating stability for her children who have experienced so many changes. She trusts God to fulfill His plan in her life; she walks with Him daily, living by faith, not by sight. Benjamin will need to start school before long. She says she doesn't know if they will have to move again. For now, they are glad to raise their boys here in L'viv.

CHAPTER ELEVEN
Marina

Marina was born in 1982 in Crimea. Her family originated from different parts of Ukraine. Her father grew up in Kherson; her grandparents came from Ivanov Frankivsk and moved to Crimea for work. Marina has one older brother Alexey. Growing up, Marina lived with her grandparents for long periods of time, because her mom was sick. Her grandma became like a mom to her, Marina said. Her grandparents had a lot of animals. Marina went to Kindergarten at an early age. She started first grade in Simferopol, living with her parents again during the school year. But the summer months were spent with Grandma. It was a wonderful time.

Her family celebrated holidays like any traditional Ukrainian family would. Her parents were not religious and would rarely go to the Orthodox church. Marina reflected that, growing up, she thought anything related to church and God was boring. Marina described her family as a typical atheistic family of the Soviet Union. Even though her family was not religious, Marina remembered that they had religious icons at home. Many Ukrainian family had these in their houses. Marina asked her grandma a little bit about God, and her grandma answered, "What you cannot see, does not exist." Marina grew up without any knowledge of God or God's word.

Marina did not like school; it was simply not interesting. She finished her high school exams but could not see herself entering the university. She took a few vocational classes, learned to be a hair dresser, especially for children, and worked after high school.

When Marina was nineteen years old, a neighbor started talking to her about God and invited her to church. She began going with her neighbor; God was clearly working in her heart. Marina had many questions about God and wanted to understand the Bible. She prayed and asked God to open her heart. As she began reading God's word, she began to understand more about God. After a month of attending church and studying the Scripture, Marina repented of her sins and became a Christian. Initially her family did not like that she was going to church. They were worried that she was involved in a cult! But her parents also saw how positively Marina's life had changed. She tried to witness to her parents, continued reading the Bible, and started to serve in the church. She also sang in the youth choir.

Her future husband, Dima, had moved to Crimea with his mother as a young college graduate. He grew up in Donetsk and had already finished a degree at Donetsk Christian University. His mother moved to Crimea to start a business; unfortunately, this enterprise failed. His mother returned to Donetsk, but Dima decided to stay in Crimea - for two reasons. First, Dima attended a church in Simferopol and enjoyed the many young people there. And second, he met Marina in 2003 at Central Baptist Church - and he was smitten. Marina liked Dima; he was tall and friendly, was easy-going and a leader; he was very likable. After dating for only one month, Dima proposed marriage.

For Marina, 2004 was an important year . She was baptized and she married Dima. Marina was twenty-one years old. She and Dima began attending a smaller church together where Dima served in the music ministry. This was a church plant from the mother church. Dima worked as a music teacher and served in the local church. Marina would set up cookies and tea to encourage people to fellowship after the service, share prayer requests, share life. She also worked in the church's summer camps, serving in the kitchen, cooking for the campers. She organized a small group for women in her home for fellowship, sharing life together and praying together. Women often shared how the fellowship with other believing women was changing their lives.

Marina and Dima soon started a family and had three sons in the space of six years. Her sons are: Sviatoslav, meaning the glory of God; Elisey, the biblical name Elisha; and Elijah, meaning the strength of God. And daughter Emma was born in L'viv in 2018; her name reminds Marina of Emmanuel, God is with us. Dima named the three boys, but it was Marina's privilege to name her daughter.

Marina was busy as a mom, homemaker, and church volunteer. The boys started elementary school in Crimea. Dima would go to work and Marina would manage the household and serve through ministries of her church. Life was good; no one anticipated any trouble. Several times a year, the family would travel to Donetsk to see family members and spend a month of summer vacation with relatives. The children would see their other grandma. Dima's parents were divorced; the kids didn't see their grandpa too often. Dima's mom also loved to travel to Crimea, see her grandchildren, and enjoy the mild climate of the most southern region of Ukraine. Many other relatives would come to visit Marina's family, as well, simply because Crimea was such a lovely place for a vacation at the sea. Marina said that they really had a lot of guests, but they had only a small apartment. How they managed the sleeping arrangements was classic Ukrainian style; people slept on the floor, more or less on top of each other. After all, free room and board *is* free room and board.

Life for Marina and her family changed drastically in 2014. Marina recalled the events with trepidation. Mysterious "green men" appeared in the streets, dressed in army uniforms, but without a country symbol to identify them. All across the city of Simferopol, war machinery and technical military supplies began to arrive. Dima had many friends who played basketball together. They noticed many soldiers, hanging out near the basketball courts. Marina explained that the city was not very large, but they saw soldiers everywhere, on every corner, and even close to their home. Soldiers were patrolling every street. Tanks and heavy armory drove into the city. The political situation in Crimea became frightening to her, Marina said.

At a local market square very near their home, soldiers rounded up people. The arrests were frightening to Marina. Dima was at work. Calling around, he talked with his friends about what to do. They all expected the situation would get worse. No one really knew what to do. Marina and Dima called some journalist friends of theirs, but they did not have any more information; everything was just happening in real time. Marina remembered that they had internet and cell phone services and were watching the events unfold on social media and their internet news agencies. It was simply horrible. Marina said they did not know how long to wait or what would happen next. In her fear, she decided to pick up her sons from school and take them home. She arrived at the elementary school and was told by the teachers that there was no reason to worry. She took the boys home anyway; she *was* worried.

It became very apparent that many mercenaries were serving among the "green men". People from other countries came to the city and did not know their way around town. They were definitely not local people, Marina said. It became more oppressive every day. Even going to karate lessons for one son became an ordeal. Then the so-called referendum took place in May 2014 to choose a new government for Crimea. The referendum was characterized by a show of force and a reaction of fear. People were afraid to do anything that would cause the authorities to notice them. Allegedly, 95.5% of the people voted for the new Russian government.

Dima realized that it was time to leave Crimea for a while. The trauma of the invasion had been stressful for both the parents and the children. The day the referendum took place, the family left. They packed the kids into the car, took a few things with them, and evacuated. The whole escape trip was stressful; getting out of Crimea was challenging, and traveling with three small children was tiring, Marina remembered. They stayed briefly with friends in Odessa, but they did not know where to go next. They had left an unstable and uncertain life in Crimea, but they had taken very few personal belongings, still thinking that they would be able to return home in a few weeks. They never thought that they would not come back.

They decided to go to Vinnytsia, as they had friends there; they could stay for a while with them. Then they traveled to Ternopol, where some other wonderful friends hosted them. Sometime later, a Christian brother invited them to use his house, located just 30 km outside of L'viv. They decided to travel and see the house, having no other option. But the house was in disrepair; they could not live there. They found an apartment in the L'viv region and rented it for a month. They needed to evaluate their situation. They had so many questions: What to do? Where to go? Was a return to Crimea possible? Where would Dima find work? What about schooling for the boys? This was in June of 2014.

Marina's mother-in-law had actually invited them earlier to come and live with her in the Donbass region. But God directed Marina and Dima toward L'viv. Marina said that after the referendum in Crimea, similar things began to happen in Donbass. The war actually started in Donbass, and the events were more violent and terrible than the events in Crimea. Dima's mom would send them photos via Viber, showing them what was going on. She would leave the area for a while, travel to Mariupol, work at the train station and try to wait it out. Many Russian troops arrived in the area of Donbass, and much technical war machinery was brought in. Donbass is now occupied territory.

By July 2014, Marina's family had moved to L'viv and rented an apartment in the city. Dima had found work as a musician in L'viv and was performing with some other Christians in a band, playing at weddings and in cafes. The kids enrolled in the school system in L'viv, but struggled initially. In Crimea, all classes had been in Russian, with one class devoted to Ukrainian language. Now, all the academic instruction was in Ukrainian. Because of the language barrier, the kids struggled with making new friends, as everyone around them spoke only Ukrainian. But even in this, God blessed them, Marina said, because after only half a year in the school system, her boys understood Ukrainian better and started to make progress in school and in their friendships with other boys. The family received some humanitarian aid from an organization called "Crimea SOS", that helped internally displaced people. They had just enough money for daily food and to pay the rent to their landlord.

Marina and her family started a new life in L'viv. Looking back, Marina said, the children did so well, and God kept everyone healthy on the journey west. Even Marina was able to find work in L'viv, taking care of an elderly lady as her companion and helper. Marina worked with this lady for three years and it supplemented the family's income. While working for this woman, Marina shared her faith in God and even read the Bible to her. It was her own small evangelism project. She saw this work as more than just an opportunity to make money; it was also a ministry for her.

After the enormous stress of fleeing from Crimea, life became almost normal again. They were living a 'new normal' now, Marina said. The kids recovered from the ordeal, Dima and Marina had steady jobs to provide for the family's needs, and school and work brought a much-appreciated rhythm to their lives again. God sent them much help, Marina reflected. People would drop off groceries, the children would receive fruit as a gift, and Dima was able to park his car in a parking garage without being charged a monthly fee. God really supported them in this trying time and helped them to find stability again after the upheaval they had been through.

Marina remembered one interesting visit of some Crimean Tatar friends to their new apartment in L'viv. The Tatar family definitely could not stay in Crimea, as persecution against this minority started almost immediately with the Russian occupation of Crimea. They were trying to move to Poland, but stopped in L'viv, and ended up living with Marina and Dima for two months. They came with their own children and a dog – it was a full house in the most literal sense imaginable. It was really a miraculous time, Marina said; finances were tight and the Tatar family could not contribute money to the household budget. Marina had to prepare food for all the household members. It was amazing how they got through this time. They were never cold, had always just enough to eat, and had a roof over their heads. Marina was glad to help others; her own exodus was so fresh in her memory.

Dima eventually decided that the family would stay permanently in L'viv. The kids showed great resilience and the parents learned from them about balancing life and regaining strength. Dima even did his driver's license test in Ukrainian, which was really stressful for him. The family of five found a new rhythm and experienced quite a few miraculous provisions from God; the children adjusted quickly to life in L'viv. They succeeded at school, as well as in their language learning. They had lived through a traumatic experience and lost their home, said Marina, but God was so faithful. She reflected on the very stressful moves, sleeping in so many temporary places, trying to keep the kids happy, healthy, and entertained. Her own struggle with the crisis and the uncertainty of the future had taken an emotional toll as well.

Marina reminisced that Crimea would always be the place where she grew up, went to school, had family and friends. But she understood now that it was not her home anymore. So much had changed in Crimea that she could not go back. She could not live with her precious family in the occupied territory. Politically, there was constant propaganda that Ukraine would become one country again. Many of Marina's friends stayed in Crimea, resigned to the occupation, learning to live with the new conditions. But Dima made it clear that he, as a musician and artist, could not live in such a controlled and confined region. The children still return to Crimea every summer for vacation, because they have close friends there. They have grandparents in Crimea and in Donetsk.

Visiting relatives in these occupied territories becomes more difficult every time they try. When Marina and the children traveled over the Ukrainian-Russian border into Crimea in the summer of 2018, they encountered problems and verbal abuse. The border guards gave them a hard time, questioning the boys about not living in Crimea, not having Russian passports. The children were intimidated and frightened. Marina had drilled them to say, "Please ask our mother; she will have answers for you." Marina kept saying, "Keep calm, boys." She kept praying that her children would not say anything offensive, leading to their arrest. Her boys did great, Marina said, and they helped her a lot with baby Emma (born 2018), who was going to meet her grandparents for the first time.

Marina's parents don't want to leave Crimea. Her father said, "I was born here, I will die here. I have a house here, I live here, I cannot leave, and I will not leave." Her parents are encountering a lot of problems right now, Marina said. Russian law is in effect. For people who hold a Ukrainian passport in contrast to the favored Russian passport, life becomes harder as they encounter prejudices and trials. Marina said that she prays for her family a lot and witnesses to them about how greatly God has worked in her life and provided for them. Marina's brother and his wife live with Marina's parents. Her brother has no desire to leave Crimea. Dima wanted to travel to Donbas to see his family, but was not able to. Dima's mom was able to visit them in L'viv three years ago.

Marina said that life in L'viv is stable now; Dima has work, the children are enrolled in a Christian school. The boys had a lot of problems at a previous school; being from a Baptist family, they did not want to learn the Catholic catechism and prayers. Marina herself is not working outside the home right now while she cares for baby Emma. She works a great deal inside the home, managing four kids, laundry, meals, and the boys' extracurricular activities. Marina said for her it is most important that her children know God, because then they will walk through any difficulties that might arise with God. She and Dima are waiting to see when God will open the boys' hearts to receive him as Lord and Savior.

In talking about their new life, Marina also mentioned that they have found a wonderful new church plant called Disciples Church. Initially, when they visited churches in L'viv, they experienced rejection and misunderstanding. People simply could not relate to them, their experiences, their current situation as refugees. Marina said that Dima was invited to give guitar lessons at the seminary, UBTS, and it just so happened that Elisey was working there. Dima found out that at the seminary a group of refugees were meeting for worship and Bible study. This information caught his interest instantly. Dima met with Elisey and asked him many questions about the church. When they visited Disciples Church for the first time, they sensed right away that this was an unusual church. They joined the small group that Elisey Pronin led, and as the church plant began to form, God sent more and more refugees to the church. Marina said it was simply amazing to see how much understanding there was between the members, because many of them had just been through the same horrific experiences Marina's family had endured in leaving Crimea.

The family began attending Disciples Church in the spring of 2016. Soon, Dima became part of the worship team for the small church plant. It was a true blessing from God in Marina's opinion, because Dima had finished musical college in Crimea and had been the worship leader in their small church. To have this ministry again in their new life in L'viv was a huge privilege and blessing. Another blessing for her was a small group meeting every week in a home for Bible study, prayer, and fellowship.

Marina said she does not know what else is coming her way, but she is thankful for the blessings and the stability that the family can enjoy right now. She is not thinking about another move, but she also has learned to be flexible, in case God should sometime move them to another place.

CHAPTER TWELVE

Epilogue

I hope you enjoyed reading *Lives Left Behind*. The testimonies of these women surely touched my heart. I am amazed at their resilience and perseverance and I admire their godly lives and their biblical worldview.

Yet there is some greater truth hidden in their stories. There is another aspect to *Lives Left Behind*. All these women know God as their Lord and Savior and are prepared to leave their lives behind — again.

You see, we will all fall into this category of a 'life left behind' one day. I don't mean just moving to another job in another city or state. One day your life on earth will be over, and you will have to leave it behind. Currently, the departure rate is 100 out of 100 people. But are you ready to leave this life behind?

When you leave your life on earth behind, you can enter a new place called heaven. But there is only one way to heaven, and Jesus said: I am the way, the truth, and the life. No one comes to the Father, except through Me. (John 14:6). God loves you and me. Our sins separate us from God. But God offers us salvation through His Son, Jesus Christ. Jesus lived a perfect, sinless life. Jesus then died on the cross for my sins and for your sins – as our substitute. By believing in Jesus, you can be saved and receive new life.

Here is a simple outline for a prayer that you might want to pray:

ABC of salvation to accept Jesus as your personal Savior:

- A—Admit that you are a sinner (Romans 3:23, Romans 6:23).
- B—Believe that Jesus is God's Son, that He died for you, and that His death can save your soul (John 3:16, Romans 5:8-10).
- C—Confess that He is your Lord and Savior (Romans 10:9-13).

My hope is that you accept Jesus Christ as your personal Lord and Savior. Life on earth will never be the same with God loving and leading you and eternal life in heaven will be your sure future destination when you leave your life behind one day. I made this decision almost 30 years ago. To God be the glory!

Ingrid Woodbridge

CHAPTER THIRTEEN

Resources

To join my mailing list and to see some videos
of the women in *Lives Left Behind,* please go to my website:

www.ingridwoodbridge.com

If you enjoyed the book, please leave a review at Amazon.

Made in USA - Kendallville, IN
1204717_9781951730000
12.03.2020 0855